The Right Moment

BY

William E. Hyche

COMMON GOOD PRESS
AUSTIN • TEXAS

www.iloveteachers.com

Inquiries should be addressed to

Common Good Press
P.O. Box 341135
Austin, Texas 78734
(512) 608-6745
www.commongoodpress.com

Library of Congress Control Number: 2001116833

ISBN 0-9709196-0-3 (soft cover)
ISBN 0-9709196-1-1 (hard cover)

Cover design by Stephen Bright

 Printed on recycled paper

Printed in the United States of America
Morgan Printing • Austin, Texas

Foreword

At some point in time you have most likely seen the bumper sticker that says, "If you can read this—thank a teacher." Teaching has been referred to as the thankless profession, but just stop and think of where we would be as individuals and as a nation if it were not for teachers. In a recent Gallop Poll, the question was asked, "Other than your parents, who had the most influence on your life?" Over 97% of the respondents said, "A teacher."

As a small token of our appreciation to you as a teacher, it is our pleasure to provide you with a copy of *The Right Moment*. Just saying "Thank you" seems minute in comparison to the hours you have spent in guiding and influencing the lives of young people. Your dedication and commitment to the betterment of our country through the education of the students in our cities, state and nation does not go unnoticed.

We sincerely hope that you enjoy the quotes and words of wisdom found on the pages of this book. Each time you read a passage, we hope you too will pause to remember one of your teachers who inspired you to become a teacher and say "Thank you."

Sincerely,

Archie E. McAfee, Executive Director
Texas Association of Secondary School Principals
Texas Association of Student Councils

Dedication

To my daughters,

Laura and Lana

Let me begin by saying I love you. I want you to know
what a privilege it is for me to have you in my life.
I want you to know what a contribution you are
to me and how you enrich my life every day by
who you are. I want you to know that I
am committed to your well-being
and to your happiness.
I am a lucky man.

Children will not remember you for the material
things you provided but for the feeling that you
cherished them.

Richard L. Evans

Acknowledgments

Perhaps the greatest social service that can be rendered by anybody to the country and to mankind is to bring up a family.

George Bernard Shaw

First I want to thank my wife Lenora, who knows a thing or two about the right moment, for her unconditional support of me and my dreams. To my parents, Edison and Ginny Hyche, for giving me abundance and raising me to believe that I can do anything. And to Lenora's parents, Wheeler and Irene Petty, for accepting me into their family and loving me like a son.

I want to acknowledge my daughter Laura, her husband Mike Shay and their wonderful sons Michael and Daniel; and my daughter Lana, her husband Jeff King and their wonderful sons Camren and Corbin. My children and their families are the light of my life. I would like to express my love and appreciation to my brothers, Gary and Mike, to my sister Becky and to their families; to Lenora's family, my extended family and to my many friends who are also my family. Your friendship and love contribute richly to my life.

Finally I want to express my gratitude to Roy Williams of the Wizard Academy, and Mark Hillis of Morgan Printing, for their integrity, vision and encouragement through the creation and production of this book.

Introduction

This book began about ten years ago as a desire to share my values with my daughters. They had left home to attend college and I missed them. I knew my daughters loved me; however, I began to wonder if they really knew what I believed and valued. So, over the next few years, I created a list of my values. This was a very significant process for me and I would recommend it. During this time, my youngest daughter, Lana, fell in love and was planning her wedding. I decided to have my value list made into a poster, have the poster framed, and give it to Laura and Lana on Lana's wedding day. This was a wonderful experience for our family and is a story unto itself.

The poster became very popular with my family and friends and I had the idea to expand the poster into a book that contained quotations that supported my value system. Over the past several years, I have collected thousands of quotations and sorted selected quotations into categories. The result of that process is this book, *The Right Moment*.

It might be well said of me that I have merely made
up a bunch of other men's flowers, and brought
nothing of my own but the string that ties them
together in a bunch, which I gladly offer to you.
Michel Eyquem de Montaigne

Compiling *The Right Moment* has been a joy for me. Thank you very much for the contribution you have made by your purchase of this book.

Bill Hyche

Table of Contents

Live so that when your children
think of fairness, caring and
integrity they think of you. . . .

Tell the Truth

But such is the irresistible nature of truth, that all
it asks, and all it wants, is the liberty of appearing.

Thomas Paine

It always comes back to the same necessity: go
deep enough and there is a bedrock of truth,
however hard.

May Sarton

One of the most striking differences between a cat
and a lie is that a cat has only nine lives.

Mark Twain

All truth passes through three stages. First, it is
ridiculed. Second, it is violently opposed. Third, it
is accepted as being self-evident.

Arthur Schopenhauer

When a situation has been dedicated wholly to
truth, peace is inevitable.

A Course in Miracles

Always carry to the rostrum a sense of the
immense consequences which may depend on
your full and faithful presentation of the truth.

R. S. Storrs

When I want to speak, let me think first. Is it
true? Is it kind? Is it necessary? If not, let it be
left unsaid.

Babcock

The unconscious wants truth. It ceases to speak to those who want something else more than truth.

Adrienne Rich

So, I simply say, what you can do personally is commit yourself to what is the truth. That's all.

Buckminster Fuller

Truth has no special time of its own. Its hour is now—always.

Albert Schweitzer

When in doubt, tell the truth.

Mark Twain

There is nothing so powerful as truth—and often nothing so strange.

Daniel Webster

Truths and roses have thorns about them.

H. G. Bohn

Honesty is the first chapter in the book of wisdom.

Thomas Jefferson

The truth is always the strongest argument.

Sophocles

Be on Time

Doest thou love life? Then do not squander time,
for that's the stuff life is made of.

Benjamin Franklin

The trouble with being punctual is that nobody's
there to appreciate it.

Franklin Jones

I've been on a calendar, but never on time.

Marilyn Monroe

Better three hours too soon than a minute too late.

William Shakespeare

Punctuality is the politeness of kings.

Louis XVIII

You may delay, but time will not.

Benjamin Franklin

Better never than late.

George Bernard Shaw

We are not saints, but we have kept our
appointment. How many people can boast as
much.

Samuel Beckett

I've wasted time, and now time doth waste me.

William Shakespeare

He who is late may gnaw the bones.

Yugoslav Proverb

I must govern the clock, not be governed by it.

Golda Meir

The ability to concentrate and use time well is everything.

Lee Iacocca

Punctuality is the soul of business.

Thomas Chandler Haliburton

To choose time is to save time.

Francis Bacon

Eighty percent of success is showing up.

Woody Allen

All time management begins with planning.

Tom Greening

Well arranged time is the surest mark of a well arranged mind.

Pitman

Until we can manage Time, we can manage nothing else.

Peter F. Drucker

Keep Your Agreements

Promises are the uniquely human way of ordering
the future, making it predictable and reliable to the
extent that this is humanly possible.

Hannah Arendt

Never promise more than you can perform.

Publilius Syrus

There were so many candidates on the platform
that there were not enough promises to go around.

Ronald Reagan

Promises and pie-crusts are made to be broken.

Jonathan Swift

Our agreements with Poland have a purely
temporary significance. I have no intention of
maintaining a serious relationship with Poland.

Adolf Hitler

A promise made is a debt unpaid.

Robert W. Service

Man's word is God in man.

Alfred Tennyson

All words, and no performance!

Philip Massinger

Democritus said words are but the shadows
of actions.

Plutarch

Treaties are like roses and young girls—they last
while they last.

Charles de Gaulle

Nothing astonishes men so much as common
sense and plain dealing.

Ralph Waldo Emerson

Words that do not match deeds are not important.

Ernesto Che Guevara

I thought he was a young man of promise; but it
appears he was a young man of promises.

Arthur Balfour

When you say that you agree to a thing in
principle, you mean that you have not the slightest
intention of carrying it out in practice.

Prince Otto von Bismark

Vows made in storms are forgotten in calms.

English Proverb

Pay Your Debts

I have discovered the philosopher's stone which
turns everything into gold. It is: "Pay as you go."

John Randolph

A small debt makes a man your debtor; a large one
makes him your enemy.

Seneca, the Elder

Debt is the worst poverty.

Thomas Fuller

When debts are not paid because they cannot be
paid, the best thing to do is not to talk about them,
and shuffle the cards again.

Camilo Jose Cela

A debt may get mouldy, but it never decays.

Chinua Achebe

It is better to pay a creditor than to give to a friend.

Aristotle

He that dies pays all debts.

William Shakespeare

If you borrow $2000 dollars from a bank and can't
pay it back, you have a problem, but if you borrow
a million and can't repay, they have a problem.

Anonymous

Dreading that climax of all human ills, the
inflammation of his weekly bills.

Lord Byron

No debts! Never borrowing! Something of freedom's
lost—and something of beauty too—from a home
that's founded on borrowing and debt.

Henrik Icahn

There are but two ways of paying debt: increase of
industry in raising income, increase of thrift in
laying out.

Thomas Carlyle

The borrower is a servant to the lender.

Proverbs 22:7

Neither a borrower nor a lender be; for loan oft
loses both itself and friend.

William Shakespeare

Let us all be happy and live within our means, even
if we have to borrow the money to do it with.

Artemus Ward

As the person who has health is young, so the
person who owes nothing is rich.

Proverb

Be Generous

We make a living from what we get; we make a life from what we give.

Winston Churchill

Real joy comes not from ease or riches or from the praise of men but from doing something worthwhile.

Wilfred T. Granfell

Giving and receiving are one in truth.

A Course in Miracles

My country is the world and my religion is to do good.

Thomas Paine

Complete possession is proved only by giving. All you are unable to give possesses you.

Andre Gide

What you deny to others will be denied to you, for the plain reason that you are always legislating for yourself; all your words and actions define the world you want to live in.

Thaddeus Golas

To receive everything, one must open one's hands and give.

Taisen Deshimaru

Do what you can, with what you have, where you are.

Theodore Roosevelt

Generous people are rarely mentally ill people.

Dr. Karl Menninger

As much as you can, strive to keep alive your compassion.

Christopher A. Rodowskas

The love we give away is the only love we keep.

Elbert Hubbard

The manner of giving is worth more than the gift.

Pierre Corneille

It is more blessed to give than to receive.

Acts 20:35

When I give, I give myself.

Walt Whitman

There's no delight in owning anything unshared.

Seneca, the Elder

The greatest pleasure I know is to do a good action by stealth, and to have it found out by accident.

Charles Lamb

Take Care of Your Spirit

We are not human beings trying to be spiritual. We are spiritual beings trying to be human.

Jacquelyn Small

Create in me a pure heart, O God, and renew a steadfast spirit within me.

Psalm 51:10

Some people get spiritual because they see the light; some get spiritual because they feel the heat. I kind of felt the heat.

Elbert Hubbard

By having a reverence for life, we enter into a spiritual relationship with the world.

Albert Schweitzer

Only the individual with a healthy, wholesome self-view will feel inwardly rich when he or she is outwardly broke.

Marsha Sinetar

Great men are they who see that spiritual is stronger than any material force; that thoughts rule the world.

Ralph Waldo Emerson

The body must be nourished, physically, emotionally and spiritually. We're spiritually starved in this culture—not underfed but undernourished.

Carol Hornig

After all, it is those who have a deep and real inner life who are best able to deal with the irritating details of outer life.

Evelyn Underhill

Safeguard the health both of body and soul.

Cleobulus

Physical strength can never permanently withstand the impact of spiritual force.

Franklin D. Roosevelt

Invest in the human soul. Who knows, it might be a diamond in the rough.

Mary McLeod Bethune

Science can point out dangers, but science cannot turn the direction of minds and hearts. That is the province of spiritual powers within and without our very beings—powers that are the mysteries of life itself.

Oren Lyons

A beautiful soul has no other merit than its existence.

Johann Friedrich Von Schiller

Give light, and darkness will disappear of itself.

Desiderius Erasmus

Take Care of Your Mind

I will not let anyone walk through my mind with their dirty feet.

Mahatma Gandhi

A man is known by the company his mind keeps.

Thomas Bailey Aldrich

If a man empties his purse into his head, no man can take it away from him. An investment in knowledge always pays the best interest.

Benjamin Franklin

The mind is its own place, and in itself can make heaven of Hell, a hell of Heaven.

John Milton

Shopping is cheaper than a psychiatrist.

Anonymous

Saying no can be the ultimate self-care.

Claudia Black

All that is comes from the mind; it is based on the mind, it is fashioned by the mind.

The Pali Canon (500-250 BC)

The devil is a gentleman who never goes where he is not welcome.

John A. Lincoln

It is not enough to have a good mind. The main thing is to use it well.

René Descartes

Nothing contributes so much to tranquilize the mind as a steady purpose—a point on which the soul may fix its intellectual eye.

Mary Wollstonecraft Shelley

The growth of the human mind is still high adventure, in many ways the highest adventure on earth.

Norman Cousins

The mind of man is capable of anything— because everything is in it, all the past as well as all the future.

Joseph Conrad

Let us train our minds to desire what the situation demands.

Seneca, the Elder

The mind is a strange machine which can combine the materials offered to it in the most astonishing ways.

Bertrand Russell

The mind is never right but when it is at peace with itself.

Seneca, the Elder

Take Care of Your Body

If you want to find the answers to the Big
Questions about your soul, you'd best begin with
the Little Answers about your body.

George Sheehan

To keep the body in good health is a
duty...otherwise we will not be able to keep our
mind strong and clear.

Buddha

If I'd known I was going to live this long, I'd have
taken better care of myself.

Eubie Blake

Wouldn't it be great if you really could work your
ass off?

Silver Rose

I will tell you what I have learned myself. For me, a
long five or six mile walk helps. And one must go
alone and every day.

Brenda Ueland

No longer conscious of my movement, I
discovered a new unity with nature. I had found
a new source of power and beauty; a source I
never dreamt existed.

Roger Bannister
(On breaking the four-minute mile)

If anything is sacred, the human body is sacred.

Walt Whitman

Here in this body are the sacred rivers: here are the sun and moon as well as all the pilgrimage places. I have not encountered another temple as blissful as my own body.

Saraha

I know from experience that the marriage of mind and body makes the sum more powerful than the individual parts.

George Foreman

Living so fully, I can't imagine what any drug could do for me.

Joan Baez

Be careful about reading health books. You may die of a misprint.

Mark Twain

The body is a sacred garment. It's your first and last garment; it is what you enter life in and what you depart life with, and it should be treated with honor.

Martha Graham

The first wealth is health.

Ralph Waldo Emerson

If the form has cracks, the spirit leaks.

Beatrice Woods

The body never lies.

Martha Graham

Forgive Others

He that cannot forgive others breaks the bridge
over which he must pass himself; for every man
has need to be forgiven.

Thomas Fuller

To be wronged is nothing unless you continue to
remember it.

Confucius

Forgive us our debts, as we forgive our debtors.

Matthew 6:12

Always forgive your enemies—nothing annoys
them so much.

Oscar Wilde

If we could read the secret history of our enemies,
we should find in each man's life sorrow and
suffering enough to disarm all hostility.

Henry Wadsworth Longfellow

The weak can never forgive. Forgiveness is the
attribute of the strong.

Mahatma Gandhi

Love truth but pardon error.

Voltaire

Man must evolve for all human conflict a method,
which rejects revenge, aggression and retaliation.
The foundation for such a method is love.

Martin Luther King, Jr.

Forgiveness is the key to action and freedom.

Hannah Arendt

He that is without sin among you, let him cast a stone at her.

John 8:7

Don't carry a grudge. While you're carrying the grudge, the other guy's out dancing.

Buddy Hackett

Never does the human soul appear so strong as when it forgoes revenge, and dares forgive any injury.

E. H. Chapin

Without forgiveness a life is governed by...an endless cycle of resentment and retaliation.

Roberto Assagioli

The act of forgiving can never be predicted: it is the only reaction that acts in an unexpected way and thus retains, though being a reaction, something of the original character of action.

Hannah Arendt

To err is human, to forgive divine.

Alexander Pope

Then said Jesus, "Father, forgive them; for they know not what they do."

Luke 23:34

Forgive Yourself

If you haven't forgiven yourself something, how can you forgive others?

Dolores Huerta

Do you mean one could be 'just angry,' with nothing extra—like a thunderstorm that comes and goes? Gosh, I wish I could do that.

Zen Master Suzuki Roshi

I can pardon everyone's mistakes but my own.

Marcos Porcius Cato

Life teaches us to be less harsh with ourselves and with others.

Goethe

There is luxury in self-reproach. When we blame ourselves, we feel no one else has the right to blame us.

Oscar Wilde

Love is an act of endless forgiveness.

Peter Ustinov

Forget and forgive. This is not difficult when properly understood. It means forget inconvenient duties, then forgive yourself for forgetting. By rigid practice and stern determination, it comes easy.

Mark Twain

Forgive yourself for your faults and your mistakes
and move on.

Les Brown

A man must learn to forgive himself.

Arthur Davison Ficke

A wise man will make haste to forgive, because he
knows the full value of time and will not suffer it
to pass away in unnecessary pain.

Rambler

We easily pardon an offense we had part in.

Juoy

Forgiveness is God's command.

Martin Luther

Forgiveness does not change the past, but it does
enlarge the future.

Paul Boese

Forgive and forget.

Proverb

The moment an individual can accept and forgive
himself, even a little, is the moment in which he
becomes to some degree lovable.

Eugene Kennedy

Forget Yourself

We are all angels with only one wing. We cannot
fly unless we embrace each other.

Luciano de Crescenzo

A human being is part of the whole that we call the
universe, a part limited in time and space. He
experiences himself, his thoughts and feelings, as
something separated from the rest—a kind of
optical illusion of his consciousness. This illusion
is a prison for us, restricting us to our personal
desires and to affection only to the few people
nearest us. Our task must be to free ourselves from
this prison by widening our circle of compassion
to embrace all living beings and all of nature.

Albert Einstein

My name used to be Me. But now it's You.

Thephane the Monk

If you want to be miserable, think about yourself,
about what you want, what you like, what respect
people ought to pay you and what people think
of you.

Charles Kingsley

An individual has not started living until he can
rise above the narrow confines of his
individualistic concerns to the broader concerns
of all humanity.

Martin Luther King, Jr.

The key to stardom is the rest of the team.

Mary Ellen Miller

Develop interest in life as you see it; in people, things, literature, music—the world is so rich, simply throbbing with rich treasures, beautiful songs, and interesting people. Forget yourself.

Henry Miller

A man wrapped up in himself makes a small bundle.

Benjamin Franklin

Study the best and highest things that are; but of yourself humble thoughts retain.

Joe Davis

If thou desire the love of God and man, be humble, for the proud heart, as it loves none but itself, is beloved of none but itself. Humility enforces where neither virtue, nor strength, nor reason can prevail.

Francis Quarles

The way a team plays as a whole determines its success. You may have the greatest bunch of individual stars in the world, but if they don't play together, the club won't be worth a dime.

Babe Ruth

Do everything with a mind that lets go. Do not expect praise or reward.

Achaan Chah

Be Kind to Everyone

My religion is very simple. My religion is kindness.

The Dalai Lama

Whoever you are—I have always depended on the kindness of strangers.

Tennessee Williams

If there is any kindness I can show, or any good thing I can do to any fellow being, let me do it now, and not deter or neglect it, as I shall not pass this way again.

William Penn

Spread love everywhere you go: first of all in your own house. Give love to your children, to your wife or husband; to a next-door neighbor…let no one ever come to you without leaving better and happier. Be the living expression of God's kindness; kindness in your face, kindness in your eyes, kindness in your smile, kindness in your warm greeting.

Mother Teresa

It is one of the most beautiful compensations of life that no man can sincerely try to help another without helping himself.

Ralph Waldo Emerson

Constant kindness can accomplish much. As the sun makes the ice melt, kindness causes misunderstandings, mistrust and hostility to evaporate.

Albert Schweitzer

I will do nothing, support nothing, or conspire with
nothing that could possibly hurt anyone or anything.

Marianne Williamson

Kindness is more important than wisdom, and the
recognition of this is the beginning of wisdom.

Theodore Isaac Rubin

Shall we make a new rule of life from tonight:
always to try to be a little kinder than is necessary.

Sir James Matthew Barrie

That best portion of a good man's life, his little,
nameless, unremembered acts of kindness and
of love.

William Wordsworth

This is the final test of a gentleman: his respect for
those who can be of no possible value to him.

William Lyon Phelps

If a man be gracious and courteous to strangers, it
shows he is a citizen of the world.

Francis Bacon

I now perceive one immense omission in my
psychology—the deepest principle of human
nature is the craving to be appreciated.

William James

No act of kindness, no matter how small, is
ever wasted.

Aesop

Expect the Best

High expectations are the key to everything.

Sam Walton

Expect your every need to be met, expect the answer to every problem, expect abundance on every level, expect to grow spiritually.

Eileen Caddy

In spite of everything, I still believe that people are really good at heart.

Anne Frank

Cats seem to go on the principle that it never does any harm to ask for what you want.

Joseph Wood Kruth

It's a funny thing about life; if you refuse to accept anything but the best, you very often get it.

Somerset Maugham

I'll go through life either first class or third, but never in second.

Noel Coward

Expect nothing, be prepared for everything.

Samurai saying

For he that expects nothing shall not be disappointed, but he that expects much—if he lives and uses that in hand day by day—shall be full to running over.

Edgar Cayce

Life.... It tends to respond to our outlook, to shape itself to meet our expectations.

Richard M. DeVos

I skate to where the puck is going to be, not where it is.

Wayne Gretzky

Other people may not have had high expectations for me...but I had high expectations for myself.

Shannon Miller

Whatever we expect with confidence becomes our own self-fulfilling prophecy.

Brian Tracy

Expect the best, plan for the worst, and prepare to be surprised.

Denis Waitley

Quality is never an accident; it is always the result of high intention, sincere effort, intelligent direction and skillful execution; it represents the wise choice of many alternatives.

William A. Foster

The best things in life are free.

Proverb

We should not let our fears hold us back from pursuing our hopes.

John F. Kennedy

Exceed Expectations

If we all did the things we are capable of doing, we would literally astound ourselves.

Thomas Edison

Our duty as men is to proceed as if limits to our ability didn't exist. We are collaborators in creation.

Tielhard de Chardin

There is no traffic jam on the extra mile.

Anonymous

When you rise in the morning, form a resolution to make the day a happy one for a fellow creature.

Sydney Smith

I am of the opinion that my life belongs to the community, and as long as I live, it is my privilege to do for it whatever I can. I want to be thoroughly used up when I die, for the harder I work, the more I live. Life is no 'brief candle' for me. It is a sort of splendid torch which I have got hold of for a moment, and I want to make it burn as brightly as possible before handing it on to future generations.

George Bernard Shaw

I shall become a master in this art only after a great deal of practice.

Erich Fromm

Hold yourself responsible for a higher standard than anyone else expects of you. Never excuse yourself.

Henry Ward Beecher

What moves men of genius, or rather what inspires
their work, is not new ideas, but their obsession
with the idea that what has already been said is still
not enough.

Eugene Delacroix

Cheat me in price, but not in the goods I purchase.

Spanish Proverb

A business that makes nothing but money is a
poor kind of business.

Henry Ford

I've got a theory that if you give 100 percent all of
the time, somehow, things will work out in the end.

Larry Bird

It never fails: Everybody who really makes it does it
by busting his ass.

Alan Arkin

If you can't win, make the fellow ahead of you
break the record.

Charles L. Tiblom

From my point of view, it is immoral for a being
not to make the most intensive effort every instant
of his life.

Ortega Y'Gasset

Produce Results

Don't tell me how hard you work. Tell me how much you get done.

James Ling

Every time we say, "Let there be!" in any form, something happens.

Stella Terrill Mann

To win one hundred victories in one hundred battles is not the acme of skill. To subdue the enemy without fighting is the acme of skill.

Sun Tzu

I don't have a lot of respect for talent. Talent is genetic. It's what you do with it that counts.

Martin Ritt

You're either part of the solution or part of the problem.

Eldridge Cleaver

I know of no more encouraging fact than the unquestionable ability of man to elevate his life by a conscious endeavor.

Henry David Thoreau

The world isn't interested in the storms you encountered but whether you brought in the ship.

Raul Armeston

Ideas are a commodity. Execution of them is not.

Michael Dell

Never mistake activity for achievement.

Mary Ellen Miller

People who say it cannot be done should not
interrupt those who are doing it.

Anonymous

What we must decide is perhaps how we are
valuable, rather than how valuable we are.

F. Scott Fitzgerald

Well done is better than well said.

Benjamin Franklin

Nothing difficult is ever easy.

Peter Badger

Nothing is to be had for nothing.

Epictetus

Surround yourself with the best people you can
find, delegate authority, and don't interfere.

Ronald Reagan

The man who gets the most satisfactory results is
not always the man with the most brilliant single
mind, but rather the man who can best coordinate
the brains and talents of his associates.

W. Alton Jones

Value Your Family

As you walk, you cut open and create that riverbed into which the stream of your descendents shall enter and flow.

Nikos Kazantzakis

What the mother sings to the cradle goes all the way down to the coffin.

Henry Ward Beecher

Allow children to be happy in their own way, for what better way will they ever find?

Dr. Johnson

Don't limit a child to your own learning, for he was born in another time.

Rabbinic saying

Home is the place where, when you have to go there, they have to take you in.

Robert Frost

When I was a boy of 14, my father was so ignorant I could hardly stand to have the old man around. But when I got to be 21, I was astonished at how much the old man had learned in seven years.

Mark Twain

Perhaps the greatest social service that can be rendered by anybody to the country and to mankind is to bring up a family.

George Bernard Shaw

Smile at each other, smile at your wife, smile at
your husband, smile at your children, smile at each
other—it doesn't matter who it is—and that will
help you grow up in greater love for each other.

Mother Teresa

No matter how much cats fight, there always seem
to be plenty of kittens.

Abraham Lincoln

From my experience and observation, if a family is
held together in difficult circumstances, nine times
out of ten it is the woman who's doing it.

Roddy Doyle

It is hazardous to shake a family tree. One never
knows what will fall out. Undesirable birds have an
impish way of roosting among the finest
genealogical branches.

Melvin Tolson

When a child is born, so are grandmothers.

Judith Levy

A man who doesn't spend time with his family can
never be a real man.

Marlon Brando

The strength of a nation derives from the integrity
of the home.

Confucius

Value Your Friends

Sometimes our light goes out but is blown into
flame by another human being. Each of us owes
deepest thanks to those who have rekindled
this light.

Albert Schweitzer

A faithful friend is a strong defense: and he that
has found such a one hath found a treasure.

Ecclesiastes 6:14

Surround yourself with people who respect and
treat you well.

Claudia Black

Love knows not its own depth until the hour
of separation.

Kahlil Gibran

If we discovered that we had only five minutes left
to say all that we wanted to say, every telephone
booth would be occupied by people calling other
people to stammer that they loved them.

Christopher Morley

There comes that mysterious meeting in life when
someone acknowledges who we are and what we
can be, igniting the circuits of our highest potential.

Rusty Berkus

To who can I speak today? I am heavy-laden with
trouble through lack of an intimate friend.

Anonymous

One loyal friend is worth ten thousand relatives.

Proverb

The only people for me are the mad ones, the ones
who are mad to live, mad to talk, mad to be saved,
desirous of everything at the same time, the ones
who never yawn or say a commonplace thing,
but burn, burn, burn like fabulous yellow
roman candles.

Jack Kerouac

Greater love has no one then this, than one lay
down his life for his friends.

John 15:13

One friend in a lifetime is much; two are many;
three are hardly possible.

Henry Adams

Each friend represents a world in us; a world
possibly not born until they arrive, and it is only
by this meeting that a new world is born.

Anais Nin

A friend is a gift you give yourself.

Robert Louis Stevenson

Perhaps this is the most important thing for me to
take back from beach living: simply the memory
that each cycle of the tide is valid, each cycle of the
wave is valid, each cycle of a relationship is valid.

Ann Morrow Lindbergh

Cherish Children

Children will not remember you for the material things you provided but for the feeling that you cherished them.

Richard L. Evans

Fifty years from now it will not matter what kind of car you drove, what kind of house you lived in, how much money you had in your bank account, or what your clothes looked like. But the world may be a little better place because you were very important in the life of a child.

Anonymous

If a child lives with approval, he learns to live with himself.

Dorothy Law Nolte

To love children is to love God.

Roy Rogers

Your children need your presence more than your presents.

Jesse Jackson

You know, I'm starting to wonder what my folks were up to at my age that makes them so doggoned suspicious of me all the time.

Margaret Blair

I have found the best way to give advice to your children is to find out what they want and then advise them to do it.

Harry S. Truman

Your children are not your children. They are the sons and daughters of Life's longing for itself.

Kahlil Gibran

A child is a guest in the house, to be loved and respected—never possessed, since he belongs to God.

J. D. Salinger

Then some children were brought to Him so that He might lay His hands on them and pray; and the disciples rebuked them. But Jesus said, "Let the children alone, and do not hinder them from coming to me; for the kingdom of heaven belongs to such as these."

Matthew 19:13-14

There are only two lasting bequests we can hope to give our children. One of these is roots; the other, wings.

Hodding Carter

Parents wonder why the streams are bitter, when they themselves have poisoned the fountain.

John Locke

Mankind owes to the child the best it has to give.

U.N. Declaration

Children need love, especially when they do not deserve it.

Harold S. Hulbert

Children are our most valuable natural resource.

Herbert Hoover

Have Clear Intentions

Undoubtedly, we become what we envisage.

Claude M. Bristol

It is no use walking anywhere to preach unless our walking is our preaching.

St. Francis of Assisi

Life is a copycat and can be bullied into following the master artist who bids it come to heel.

Heywood Broun

If you don't know where you are going, you will probably end up somewhere else.

Laurence Johnson Peter

I am in the world only for the purpose of composing.

Franz Schubert

I find the great thing in this world is, not so much where we stand, as in what direction we are moving.

Goethe

I expect to spend the rest of my life in the future so I want to be reasonably sure what kind of future it's going to be. That is my reason for planning.

Charles Kettering

We are all pencils in the hand of God.

Mother Theresa

Once you get rid of the idea that you must please other people before you please yourself, and you begin to follow your own insticnts—*only* then can you be successful. You become more satisfied, and when you are, other people tend to be satisfied by what you do.

Raquel Welch

One must not lose desires. They are mighty stimulants to creativeness, to love and to long life.

Alexander Bogomoletz

Doubt is the result of conflicting wishes. Be sure of what you want and doubt becomes impossible.

A Course in Miracles

Destiny is not a matter of chance, it is a matter of choice; it is not a thing to be waited for, it is a thing to be achieved.

William Jennings Bryan

Measure a thousand times and cut once.

Proverb

Establishing goals is all right if you don't let them deprive you of interesting detours.

Doug Larson

Hell is paved with good intentions, not with bad ones. All men mean well.

George Bernard Shaw

Stay on Purpose

The purpose of life is a life of purpose.

Robert Byrne

I have always known that at last I would take this
road, but yesterday I did not know that it would
be today.

Narihira

This is the true joy of life, the being used for a
purpose recognized by yourself as a mighty one;
the being a force of nature instead of a feverish
little clod of ailments and grievances complaining
that the world will not devote itself to making
you happy.

George Barnard Shaw

We are what we repeatedly do. Excellence, then, is
not an act but a habit.

Aristotle

Nothing tastes as good as thin feels.

Weight Watchers

Character cannot be developed in ease and quiet.
Only through experiences of trial and suffering can
the soul be strengthened, vision cleared, ambition
inspired and success achieved.

Helen Keller

Don't compromise yourself; you are all you've got.

Betty Ford

When you get right down to the root meaning of the word "succeed", you find it simply means to follow through.

F. W. Nichol

The secret of success is constancy to purpose.

Benjamin Disraeli

A man like me cannot live without a hobbyhorse, a consuming passion—in Schiller's words a tyrant. I have found my tyrant, and in his service I know no limits. My tyrant is psychology.

Sigmund Freud

If a man hasn't discovered something that he will die for, he isn't fit to live.

Martin Luther King, Jr.

If you want to be successful, know what you are doing, love what you are doing and believe in what you are doing.

Will Rogers

The first thing to do in life is to do with purpose what one purposes to do.

Pablo Casals

You can come to understand your purpose in life by slowing down and feeling your heart's desires.

Marcia Wieder

Never Give Up

Nothing in the world can take the place of perseverance. Talent will not; nothing is more common than unsuccessful men with talent. Genius will not; unrewarded genius is almost a proverb. Persistence and determination alone are omnipotent.

Calvin Coolidge

In the depth of winter, I finally learned that within me there lay an invincible summer.

Albert Camus

Failure is simply the opportunity to begin again, this time more intelligently.

Henry Ford

There is nothing I like so much as a good fight.

Franklin D. Roosevelt

When a true genius appears in the world, you may know him by this sign: that all the dunces in the world are in confederation against him.

Jonathon Swift

Years may wrinkle the skin, but to give up enthusiasm wrinkles the soul.

Samuel Ullman

History has noted that the most notable winners usually encounter heartbreaking obstacles before they triumphed. They won because they refused to become discouraged by their defeats.

B. C. Forbes

The promise land always lies on the other side of a wilderness.

Havelock Ellis

There is no such thing as a great talent without great willpower.

Honoree de Balzac

Effort only fully realizes its reward after a person refuses to quit.

Napoleon Hill

In the middle of difficulty lies opportunity.

Albert Einstein

It's a long old road, but I know I'm gonna find the end.

Bessie Smith

It ain't over 'til it's over.

Yogi Berra

There has never been a great athlete who died not knowing what pain is.

Bill Bradley

What doesn't kill me makes me stronger.

Albert Camus

Thousands of people have talent. The one and only thing that counts is: Do you have staying power?

Noel Coward

Be Responsible

Take your life in your own hands and what
happens? A terrible thing: no one to blame.

Erica Jong

To accept the responsibility of being a child of God
is to accept the best that life has to offer you.

Stella Terrill Mann

Each new day is a gift from God. How you live it is
your gift to Him.

Anonymous

You become responsible forever for what you
have tamed.

Antoine de Saint-Exupery

I wish people would realize that animals are totally
dependent, helpless, like children; a trust that is
put upon us.

James Herriot

There is no tougher challenge that we face than to
accept personal responsibility for not only what we
are but also what we can be.

David McNally

Choice of attention—to pay attention to this and
ignore that—is to the inner life what choice of
action is to the outer. In both cases, a man is
responsible for his choice and must accept the
consequences.

W. H. Auden

And life is what we make it, always has been,
always will be.

Grandma Moses

This is the fire that will help the generations to
come if they use it in a sacred manner. But if they
do not use it well, the fire will have the power to do
them great harm.

Sioux Indian

Have you ever met a man so small that he could
hide behind a technicality?

Roy H. Willimas

Do what you can, with what you have, with where
you are.

Theodore Roosevelt

Unto whomsoever much is given, of him shall
much be required.

Luke 12:48

The first responsibility of a leader is to define
reality. The last is to say thank you.

Max de Pree

The buck stops here.

Harry S. Truman

Immense power is acquired by assuring yourself
in your secret reveries that you were born to
control affairs.

Andrew Carnegie

Learn to Communicate

Who you are speaks so loudly that I can't hear
what you're saying.

Ralph Waldo Emerson

Mastery of language affords remarkable power.

Frantz Fanon

Drawing on my fine command of language, I
said nothing.

Robert Benchley

Tact is the unsaid part of what you think.

Winston Churchill

Have something to say and say it as clearly as you
can. That is the only secret of style.

Matthew Arnold

There are four ways, and only four ways, in which
we have contact with the world. We are evaluated
and classified by these four contacts: what we do,
how we look, what we say, and how we say it.

Dale Carnegie

Effective communication between parties is all but
impossible if each plays to the gallery.

Roger Fisher and William Ury
(Getting to Yes)

Conversation has a kind of charm about it, an
insinuating and insidious something that elicits
secrets from us just like love or liquor.

Seneca, the Younger

He talked and talked because he didn't know what
to say.

Dacia Maraini

A word from the heart goes straight to the heart.

Abbé Huvelin

The voice of the intellect is a soft one, but it does
not rest until it has gained a hearing.

Sigmund Freud

When the eyes say one thing, and the tongue
another, a practiced man relies on the language of
the first.

Ralph Waldo Emerson

When you are a bear of very little brain and you
think of things, you find sometimes that a thing
which seemed very thingish inside you is quite
different when it gets out into the open and has
other people looking at it.

A.A. Milne

It is generally better to deal by speech than by letter.

Francis Bacon

The music that can deepest reach, and cure all ill, is
cordial speech.

Ralph Waldo Emerson

The art of communication is the language
of leadership.

James Humes

Learn to Listen

All you need to do to receive guidance is to ask for it and then listen.

Sanaya Roman

At a certain point you say to the woods, to the sea, to the mountains, the world. Now I am ready. Now I will stop and be wholly attentive. You empty yourself and wait, listening. After a time you hear it: There is nothing there...you feel the world's word as a tension, a hum, a single chorused note everywhere the same. This is it: this hum is the silence.

Annie Dillard

When your heart speaks, take good notes.

Anonymous

The first duty of love is to listen.

Paul Tillich

Listening is a form of accepting.

Stella Terrill Mann

One of the most valuable things we can do to heal one another is listen to each other's stories.

Rebecca Falls

Listening, not imitation, may be the sincerest form of flattery.

Joyce Brothers

There are voices which we hear in solitude, but they grow faint and inaudible as we enter into the world.

Ralph Waldo Emerson

Give every man thine ear, but few thy voice.

William Shakespeare

A good listener is not only popular everywhere,
but after a while, knows something.

Wilson Mizner

You can't fake listening. It shows.

Raquel Welch

Often I am still listening when the song is over.

Jean Francois Saint-Lambert

Hear the other side.

Saint Augustine of Hippo

The emergence and blossoming of understanding,
love and intelligence has nothing to do with any
tradition, no matter how ancient or impressive—it
has nothing to do with time. It happens completely
on its own when a human being questions,
wonders, listens and looks without getting stuck in
fear, pleasure and pain. When self-concern is quiet,
in abeyance, heaven and earth are open. The
mystery, the essence of all life is not separate from
the silent openness of simple listening.

Toni Packer

A closed mouth catches no flies.

Miguel de Cervantes

The older I grow, the more I listen to people who
don't talk much.

Germain G. Glidden

Be Brief

Talk low, talk slow, and don't say too much.

John Wayne

Brevity is the soul of wit.

William Shakespeare

The fewer the words, the better the prayer.

Martin Luther

Say nothing often.

Anonymous

The most valuable of all talents is that of never
using two words when one will do.

Thomas Jefferson

The great seal of truth is simplicity.

Herman Boerhaave

For parlor use, the vague generality is a life saver.

George Ade

Good things, when short, are twice as good.

Baltasar Gracian

Brevity and conciseness are the parents
of correction.

Hosea Ballou

Two monologues do not make a dialogue.

Jeff Daly

In art, economy is always beauty.

Henry James

My father gave me these hints on speech-making:
"Be sincere...be brief...be seated."

James Roosevelt

Promise is most given when the least is said.

George Chapman

Men are born with two eyes, but one tongue, in
order that they should see twice as much as
they say.

Charles Caleb Colton

All pleasantry should be short; and it might even
be as well were the serious short also.

Voltaire

You can suffocate a thought by expressing it with
too many words.

Frank A. Clark

If you would be pungent, be brief; for it is with
words as with sunbeams. The more they are
condensed, the deeper they burn.

Robert Southey

If it takes a lot of words to say what you have in
mind, give it more thought.

Dennis Roth

Be Bold

The big question is whether you are going to be
able to say a hearty yes to your adventure.

Joseph Campbell

Whatever you can do or dream, you can begin it.
Boldness has genius, power and magic in it.

Goethe

We cannot put off living until we are ready. The
most salient characteristic of life is its coerciveness:
it is always urgent, here and now, without any
possible postponement. Life is fired at us
point blank.

Ortega Y'Gasset

God always gives us strength enough, and sense
enough, for everything He wants us to do.

John Ruskin

He was a bold man that first ate an oyster.

Jonathan Swift

Don't be afraid to take big steps. You can't cross a
chasm in two jumps.

David Lloyd George

Behold the turtle. He makes progress only when he
sticks his neck out.

James B. Conant

Be bold when you've got a hot hand.

Charles H. Kirbo

We will not know unless we begin.

Howard Zinn

That's one small step for man, one giant leap
for mankind.

Neil Armstrong

Fortune befriends the bold.

John Dryden

When you cannot make up your mind which of
two evenly balanced courses of action you should
take—choose the bolder.

William Joseph Slim

Act boldly and unseen forces will come to your aid.

Dorothea Brande

When a resolute young fellow steps up to the great
bully, the world, and takes him boldly by the beard,
he is often surprised to find it comes off in his
hand, and that it was only tied on to scare away the
timid adventurers.

Ralph Waldo Emerson

Continue to Grow

The most violent element in society is ignorance.

Emma Goldman

Even when walking in a party of no more than three, I can always be certain of learning from those I am with. There will be good qualities that I can select for imitation and bad ones that will teach me what requires correction in myself.

Confucius

The greatest revolution of our generation is the discovery that human beings, by changing the inner attitudes of their minds, can change the outer aspects of their lives.

William James

Man can learn nothing except by going from the known to the anonymous.

Claude Bernard

He who is not busy being born is busy dying.

Bob Dylan

You don't have to be sick to be better.

Anonymous

To read well, that is to read true books in a true spirit, is a noble exercise.

Henry David Thoreau

When I get a little money I buy books; and if any is left I buy food and clothes.

Desiderius Erasmus

Real learning comes about when the competitive spirit has ceased.

J. Krishnamurti

We learn something by doing it. There is no other way.

John Holt

Knowledge is power.

Francis Bacon

Man's mind once stretched by a new idea, never regains its original dimension.

Oliver Wendell Holmes

The man who views the world at 50 the same as he did at 20 has wasted 30 years of his life.

Muhammad Ali

To teach well is to be a lifelong student.

Johnetta Betsch Cole

No tool is more beneficial than intelligence. No enemy is more harmful than ignorance.

Sheikh al-Mufid

Education is not filling a bucket but lighting a flame.

William Butler Yeats

The only person who is educated is the one who has learned how to learn...and change.

Carl Rogers

Serve

I don't know what your destiny will be, but one
thing I do know: the only ones among you who
will be really happy are those who have sought and
found how to serve.

Albert Schweitzer

It is within my power either to serve God or not to
serve him. Serving him, I add to my own good and
the good of the whole world. Not serving him, I
forfeit my own good and deprive the world of that
good, which was in my power to create.

Leo Tolstoy

The service we render others is really the rent we
pay for our room on the earth.

Sir Wilfred Grenfell

Everybody can be great because anybody can serve.
You don't have to have a college degree to serve.
You don't have to make your subject and verb
agree to serve. You only need a heart full of grace.
A soul generated by love.

Martin Luther King, Jr.

There is no higher religion than human service. To
work for the common good is the greatest creed.

Albert Schweitzer

No one is useless in this world who lightens the
burden of another.

Charles Dickens

I am only one. But still, I am one. I cannot do everything, but still I can do something. And because I cannot do everything, I will not refuse to do the something that I can do.

Edward Everett Hale

So long as we love, we serve; so long as we are loved by others, I would almost say we are indispensable; and no man is useless while he has a friend.

Robert Louis Stevenson

I touch the future. I teach.

Christa McAuliffe

A teacher affects eternity.

Henry Brooks Adams

A man is called selfish not for pursuing his own good, but for neglecting his neighbors.

Richard Whately

The best way to find yourself is to lose yourself in the service of others.

Mahatma Gandhi

The high destiny of the individual is to serve rather than to rule.

Albert Einstein

Think

The soul becomes dyed with the color of
its thoughts.

Marcus Aurelius

As a man thinketh, so is he, and as man chooseth,
so is he.

Bible

The real problem is not whether machines think
but whether men do.

Burrhus Frederic Skinner

The unleashed power of the atom has changed
everything save our modes of thinking, and thus
we drift toward unparalleled catastrophes.

Albert Einstein

The next empires will be in the mind.

Winston Churchill

Thus the task is not so much to see what no one
yet has seen, but to think what nobody yet has
thought about that which everybody sees.

Schopenhauer

The highest possible stage in mortal culture is
when we recognize that we ought to control our
thoughts.

Charles Darwin

To act is easy; to think is hard.

Goethe

Keep up the fires of thought and all will go
well...You fail in your thoughts or you prevail in
your thoughts alone.

Henry David Thoreau

It is the habitual thought that frames itself into our
life. It affects us even more than our intimate social
relationships do. Our confidential friends have not
so much to do in shaping our lives as the thoughts
which we harbor.

J. W. Teal

Change your thoughts and you change your world.

Norman Vincent Peale

I think, therefore I am.

René Descartes

A public-opinion poll is no substitute for thought.

Warren Buffett

Thought takes a man out of servitude, into freedom.

Henry Wadsworth Longfellow

Nothing is good or bad, but thinking makes it so.

William Shakespeare

Man is the product of his thoughts; what he
thinks, he becomes.

Mahatma Gandhi

Be Positive

I figured that if I said it enough, I would convince the world that I really was the greatest.

Muhammad Ali

We have been taught to believe that negative equals realistic and positive equals unrealistic.

Susan Jeffers

Sour grapes can ne'er make sweet wine.

Thomas Fuller

I seldom think about my limitations and they never make me sad. Perhaps there is just a touch of yearning at times; but it is vague, like a breeze among flowers.

Helen Keller

Too many people ruin what could be a happy day by dwelling on a lost yesterday and in this way jeopardize tomorrow.

Ursula Bloom

Wisdom entereth not into a malicious mind.

Rabelias

Whether you think you can or think you can't, you're right.

Henry Ford

I will speak ill of no man, and speak all the good I know of everybody.

Benjamin Franklin

Hope is the feeling you have that the feeling you have isn't permanent.

Jean Kerr

Positive thinking is the key to success in business, education, pro football, anything that you can mention. I go out there thinking that I'm going to complete every pass.

Ron Jaworski

I am optimistic and confident in all that I do. I affirm only the best for myself and others. I am the creator of my life and my world. I meet daily challenges gracefully and with complete confidence. I fill my mind with positive, nurturing, and healing thoughts.

Alice Potter

Positiveness is a good quality for preachers and speakers because, whoever shares his thoughts with the public will convince them as he himself appears convinced.

Jonathon Swift

I can't believe that God put us on this earth to be ordinary.

Lou Holtz

Nothing can stop the man with the right mental attitude from achieving his goal; nothing on earth can help the man with the wrong mental attitude.

W. W. Ziege

Don't Worry

Since everything is but an apparition, perfect in
being what it is, having nothing to do with good or
bad, acceptance or rejection, one may well burst
out in laughter.

Long Chen Pa

Look at the lilies and the way they grow. They do
not toil. They do not spin. Yet I tell you, even King
Solomon in all his glory was never dressed as
wonderfully as these.

Luke 12:27

Let us be of good cheer, remembering that the
misfortunes hardest to bear are those which
never happen.

James Russell Lowell

Difficult times have helped me to understand better
than before how infinitely rich and beautiful life is
in every way and that so many things that one goes
worrying about are of no importance whatsoever.

Isak Dinesen

Few problems are so big that they cannot be
successfully ignored.

Roy H. Williams

When I am all hassled about something, I always
stop and ask myself what difference it will make in
the evolution of the human species in the next ten
million years, and that question always helps me to
get back my perspective.

Anne Wilson Schaef

We are not troubled by things, but by the opinions which we have of things.

Epictetus

Concern should drive us into action and not into a depression.

Karen Horney

I have no regrets. I wouldn't have lived my life the way I did if I was going to worry about what people were going to say.

Ingrid Bergman

The secret of not having worries, for me at least, is to have ideas.

Eugene Delacroix

Therefore, do not worry about tomorrow, for tomorrow will worry about itself. Each day has enough trouble of its own.

Matthew 6:34

I have learned to live each day as it comes, and not to borrow trouble by dreading tomorrow. It is the dark menace of the future that makes cowards of us.

Dorothy Dix

A mistake in judgment isn't fatal, but too much anxiety about judgment is.

Pauline Kael

Worry is the interest paid on trouble before it falls due.

W. R. Inge

Don't Procrastinate

Procrastination is the natural assassin
of opportunity.

Anonymous

You cannot escape the responsibility of tomorrow
by evading it today.

Abraham Lincoln

If you were going to die soon and had only one
phone call you could make, who would you call and
what would you say? And why are you waiting?

Stephen Levine

Procrastination is the art of keeping up
with yesterday.

Don Marquis

In delay there lies no plenty.

William Shakespeare

Procrastination is the thief of time.

Edward Young

Good that comes too late is good for nothing.

Anonymous

We will not know unless we begin.

Howard Zinn

The bitterest tears shed over graves are for words
left unsaid and deeds left undone.

Harriet Beecher Stowe

Let us make hay while the sun shines.

Miguel de Cervantes

Life, as it is called, is for most of us one
long postponement.

Henry Miller

What may be done at any time will be done at
no time.

Thomas Fuller

I was taught that the way of progress is neither
swift nor easy.

Marie Curie

Never put off till tomorrow what you can do the
day after tomorrow.

Mark Twain

Never leave that till tomorrow which you can
do today.

Benjamin Franklin

There is nothing so fatal to character as half
finished tasks.

David Lloyd George

Don't wait. The time will never be just right.

Napoleon Hill

Be Still

Most of the evils in life arise from man's being
unable to sit still in a room.

Blaise Pascal

A mind too active is no mind at all.

Theodore Roethke

Learn to get in touch with the silence within
yourself and know that everything in this life has
a purpose.

Elisabeth Kubler-Ross

We are always doing something, talking, reading,
listening to the radio, and planning what next. The
mind is kept naggingly busy on some easy,
unimportant external thing all day.

Brenda Ueland

The holiest of all holidays are those kept by
ourselves in silence and apart; the secret
anniversaries of the heart.

Henry Wadsworth Longfellow

No trumpets sound when the important decisions
of our life are made. Destiny is made known silently.

Agnes de Mille

When real silence is dared, we can come very close
to ourselves and to the deep center of the world.

James Carroll

Quiet minds cannot be perplexed or frightened,
but go on in fortune or misfortune at their own
private pace, like a clock in a thunderstorm.

Robert Louis Stevenson

Be still and know that I am God.

Psalm 46:10

We must reserve a back shop all our own, entirely
free, in which to establish our real liberty and our
principle retreat and solitude.

Michel Eyquem de Montaigne

Go placidly amid the noise and haste and
remember what peace there may be in silence.

Desiderata

All you need is deep within you waiting to unfold
and reveal itself. All you have to do is be still and
take time to seek for what is within, and you will
surely find it.

Eileen Caddy

The daily pressures to act, to do, to decide, make it
difficult to stop and think, to consider, and to
examine your life goals, directions and priorities—
to find the best choices you have for managing
your own world.

Roy Menninger

Pray

My greatest weapon is mute prayer.

Mahatma Gandhi

Your desire is your prayer. Picture the fulfillment
of your desire now and feel its reality and you will
experience the joy of answered prayer.

Dr. Joseph Murphy

Our prayers should be for blessings in general, for
God knows best what is good for us.

Socrates

The strength and happiness of a man consists in
finding out the way in which God is going, and
going that way too.

Henry Ward Beecher

More things are wrought by prayer than this world
dreams of.

Alfred Lord Tennyson

A prayer in its simplest definition is merely a wish
turned God-ward.

Phillips Brooks

Hands to work, hearts to God.

Shaker axiom

We all have angels guiding us.... They look after
us. They heal us, touch us, comfort us with
invisible warm hands... What will bring their
help? Asking. Giving thanks.

Sophy Burnham

If you believe, you will receive whatever you ask for in prayer.

Matthew 21:22

The family that prays together stays together.

Anonymous

Work as if you were to live a hundred years. Pray as if you were to die tomorrow.

Benjamin Franklin

Let everyone try and find that as a result of daily prayer he adds something new to his life, something with which nothing can be compared.

Mahatma Gandhi

The men who have guided the destiny of the United States have found the strength for their tasks by going to their knees. This private unity of public men and their God is an enduring source of reassurance for the people of America.

Lyndon B. Johnson

We are all weak, finite, simple human beings, standing in the need of prayer. None need it so much as those who think they are strong, those who know it not, but are deluded by self-sufficiency.

Harold C. Phillips

Do not make prayer a monologue—make it a conversation.

Anonymous

Participate

All life is an experiment. The more experiments
you make, the better.

Ralph Waldo Emerson

God helps them that helps themselves.

Benjamin Franklin

There is no failure except in no longer trying.

Elbert Hubbard

In love there is always one who kisses and one who
offers the cheek.

French Proverb

Bad officials are elected by good citizens who do
not vote.

George Jean Nathan

People who never get carried away should be.

Malcolm Forbes

The most important thing in the Olympic Games
is not winning but taking part.... The essential
thing in life is not conquering but fighting well.

Pierre de Coubertin

One never notices what has been done; one can
only see what remains to be done.

Marie Curie

The distance doesn't matter; it is only the first step
that is the most difficult.

Marie du Deffand

Nature gave men two ends—one to sit on, and one to
think with. Ever since then, man's success or failure
has been dependent on the one he used most.

George R. Kirkpatrick

In a world where there is so much to be done, I felt
strongly impressed that there must be something
for me to do.

Dorothea Dix

A bird doesn't sing because it has an answer, it
sings because it has a song.

Maya Angelou

It is easy to sit up and take notice. What is difficult
is getting up and taking action.

Al Batt

You can't aim a duck to death.

Gael Boardman

Someone's sitting in the shade today because
someone planted a tree a long time ago.

Warren Buffett

Jump into the middle of things, get your hands
dirty, fall flat on your face, and then reach for
the stars.

Joan L. Curcio

The truth of the matter is that you always know
the right thing to do. The hard part is doing it.

Norman Schwarkzopf

Hold Yourself Accountable

No one can make you feel inferior without
your consent.

Eleanor Roosevelt

If you want good customer service, be a
good customer.

Bill Hyche

The hottest place in Hell is reserved for those who
in times of crisis preferred to remain neutral.

Dante

The unfortunate thing about this world is that
good habits are so much easier to give up than
bad ones.

Somerset Maugham

People are always blaming their circumstances for
what they are. I don't believe in circumstances. The
people who get on in this world are the people
who get up and look for the circumstances they
want, and, if they can't find them, make them.

George Bernard Shaw

It's harder to conceal ignorance than to
acquire knowledge.

Arnold H. Glasow

I never wonder to see men wicked, but I often
wonder to see them not ashamed.

Jonathon Swift

It is quite gratifying to feel guilty if you haven't done anything wrong: how noble! Whereas it is rather hard and certainly depressing to admit guilt and repent.

Hannah Arendt

Some people have greatness thrust upon them. Very few have excellence thrust upon them.

John Gardner

Now that it's all over, what did you do yesterday that's worth mentioning?

Coleman Cox

A man who has committed a mistake and doesn't correct it, is committing another mistake.

Confucius

The proactive approach to a mistake is to acknowledge it instantly, correct and learn from it. This literally turns a failure into a success.

Stephen R. Covey

If you want to be happy, put your effort into controlling the sail, not the wind.

Anonymous

Nobody can do it for you.

Ralph Cordiner

Do the Right Thing

It's the action, not the fruit of the action, that's important. You have to do the right thing. It may not be in your power; may not be in your time, that there'll be any fruit. But that doesn't mean you stop doing the right thing. You may never know what results come from your action. But if you do nothing, there will be no result.

Mahatma Gandhi

It is easy to make a dollar but it is hard to make a difference.

Kevin Kelly

Never doubt that a small group of concerned citizens can change the world. Indeed, it is the only thing that ever has.

Margaret Mead

Humanity is outraged in me and with me. We must not dissimulate nor try to forget this indignation, which is one of the most passionate forms of love.

George Sand

Maybe a person's time would be as well spent raising food as raising money to buy food.

Frank A. Clark

It takes less time to do a right thing than to explain why you did it wrong.

Henry Wadsworth Longfellow

In matters of style, swim with the current; in
matters of principle, stand like a rock.

Thomas Jefferson

Few men have virtue to withstand the highest bidder.

George Washington

When you were born, you cried and the world
rejoiced. Live your life in such a manner that when
you die the world cries and you rejoice.

Old Indian saying

Integrity is so perishable in the summer months
of success.

Vanessa Redgrave

Hide nothing from the masses of our people. Tell
no lies. Expose lies whenever they are told. Mask
no difficulties, mistakes, failures. Claim no
easy victories.

Amilcar Cabral

It is better to follow the Voice inside and be at war
with the whole world, than to follow the ways of
the world and be at war with your deepest self.

Michael Pastore

The superior man understands what is right; the
inferior man understands what will sell.

Confucius

Protect Planet Earth

Is civilization progress? The challenge, I think, is
clear; and, as clearly, the final answer will be given
not by our amassing of knowledge, or by the
discoveries of our science, or by the speed of our
aircraft, but by the affect our civilized activities
have upon the quality of our planet's life—the life
of plants and animals as well as that of men.

Charles A. Lindbergh, Jr.

The clearest way into the Universe is through a
forest wilderness.

John Muir

We are going to have to find ways of organizing
ourselves cooperatively, sanely, scientifically,
harmonically, and in regenerative spontaneity with
the rest of humanity around earth.... We are not
going to be able to operate our spaceship earth
successfully nor for much longer unless we see it as
a whole spaceship and our fate as common. It has
to be everybody or nobody.

Buckminster Fuller

There is sufficiency in the world for man's need
but not for man's greed.

Mahatma Gandhi

The magnificence of mountains, the serenity of
nature—nothing is safe from the idiot marks of
man's passing.

Loudon Wainwright

In wilderness is the preservation of the world.

Henry David Thoreau

Man has lost the capacity to foresee and forestall.
He will end by destroying the earth.

Albert Schweitzer

The wild places are where we began. When they
end, so do we.

David Brower

We won't have a society if we destroy
the environment.

Margaret Mead

When one tugs at a single thing in nature, he finds
it attached to the rest of the world.

John Muir

Take what you can use and let the rest go by.

Ken Kesey

We are all passengers aboard one ship, the earth,
and we must not allow it to be wrecked. There will
be no second Noah's Ark.

Mikhail Gorbachev

We do not inherit the land from our ancestors; we
borrow it from our children.

Native American Proverb

Make Decisions

When you come to a fork in the road, take it.

Yogi Berra

Whenever I have to choose between two evils. I
always like to try the one I haven't tried before.

Mae West

Justice delayed is justice denied.

William Ewart Gladstone

Not to decide is to decide.

Harvey Cox

If you have more than one, you don't have any.

John Madden

The difficulty in life is the choice.

George Moore

If you don't stand for something, you'll fall
for anything.

Anonymous

It's better to be boldly decisive and risk being
wrong than to agonize at length and be right
too late.

Marilyn Moats Kennedy

I have had enough.

Golda Meir

I discovered I always have choices and sometimes it's only a choice of attitude.

Judith M. Knowlton

The two important things I did learn were that you are as powerful and strong as you allow yourself to be, and that the most difficult part of any endeavor is taking the first step, making the first decision.

Robyn Davidson

Delay always breeds danger.

Miguel de Cervantes

He who hesitates is a damn fool.

Mae West

Nothing is more difficult, and therefore more precious, than to be able to decide.

Napoleon Bonaparte

Once you make a decision, the universe conspires to make it happen.

Ralph Waldo Emerson

Decision is a sharp knife that cuts clean and straight. Indecision is a dull one that hacks and tears and leaves ragged edges behind.

Jan McKeithen

Consider the Consequences

You can do anything in this world if you are
prepared to take the consequences.

Somerset Maugham

Praise Allah, but first tie your camel to a post.

Sufi saying

The cost of a thing is the amount of what I call life
which is required to be exchanged for it,
immediately or in the long run.

Henry David Thoreau

No man can put a chain about the ankle of his
fellow man without at last finding the other end
fastened about his own neck.

Frederick Douglas

You shall have joy or you shall have power, said
God; you shall not have both.

Ralph Waldo Emerson

The great masses of the people will more easily fall
victims to a big lie than to a small one.

Adolf Hitler

You are free to believe what you choose, and what
you do attest to what you believe.

A Course in Miracles

The cautious seldom err.

Confucius

The past is not a package one can lay away.

Emily Dickinson

He who drinks boilermakers tonight will hear the noise of construction work in the morning.

John Kilsea

Man is the only animal that can be skinned more than once.

Jimmy Durante

We are now discussing embedded processors to connect our refrigerators to bathroom scales and the grocery store, yet many children in the world go to bed hungry at night.

Bill Robinson

Study the past, if you would divine the future.

Confucius

But words once spoke can never be recalled.

Wentworth Dillon

He who passively accepts evil is as much involved in it as he who helps to perpetrate it.

Martin Luther King, Jr.

Be Brave

I had felt for a long time, that if I was ever told to get up so a white person could sit, that I wouldn't do it.

Rosa Parks

I cannot and I will not cut my conscience to fit this year's fashion.

Lillian Hellman

The world has achieved brilliance without conscience. Ours is a world of nuclear giants and ethical infants.

Omar Bradley

Whenever I hear someone arguing for slavery, I feel a strong impulse to see it tried on him personally.

Abraham Lincoln

Life shrinks or expands in proportion to one's courage.

Anais Nin

One man with courage makes a majority.

Andrew Jackson

Once you have done the mental work, there comes a point you have to throw yourself into the action and put your heart on the line. That means not only being brave, but being passionate toward yourself, your teammates and your opponents.

Phil Jackson

The basic difference between an ordinary man and a warrior is that a warrior takes everything as a challenge, while an ordinary man takes everything either as a blessing or a curse.

Don Juan

With courage you will dare to take risks, have the strength to be compassionate and the wisdom to be humble. Courage is the foundation of integrity.

Keshavan Nair

It is easier to fight for one's principles than to live up to them.

Alfred Adler

Those who are going to be in business tomorrow are those who understand that the future, as always, belongs to the brave.

William Bernbach

We must travel in the direction of our fear.

John Berryman

Sacred cows make the tastiest hamburger.

Abbie Hoffman

Courage is contagious. When a brave man takes a stand, the spines of others are often stiffened.

Billy Graham

Have Faith

Without faith nothing is possible. With it, nothing
is impossible.

Mary McLeod Bethune

Success is going from failure to failure without
losing enthusiasm.

Winston Churchill

Living is a form of not being sure, not knowing
what next or how. The moment you know how,
you begin to die a little. The artist never entirely
knows. We guess. We may be wrong, but we take
leap after leap in the dark.

Agnes de Mille

Embrace Tiger, Return to Mountain.

Old Chinese saying

I do not seek to understand so that I may believe,
but I believe so that I may understand.

Saint Anselm

For we walk by faith, not by sight.

II Corinthians 5:7

I feel no need for any other faith than my faith in
human beings.

Pearl S. Buck

Leap, and the net will appear.

Julie Cameron

I believe though I do not comprehend, and I hold
by faith what I cannot grasp with the mind.

St. Bernard

I have no way of knowing what results my actions
will have.... My only sure reward is in my actions
and not from them. The quality of my reward is in
the depth of my response.

Hugh Prather

It is only by living completely in this world that
one learns to have faith.

Dietrich Bonhoeffer

Our faith comes in moments... yet there is a depth in
those brief moments which constrains us to ascribe
more reality to them than to all other experiences.

Ralph Waldo Emerson

Getting ahead in a difficult profession requires
avid faith in yourself. You must be able to sustain
yourself against staggering blows. There is no code
of conduct to help beginners. That is why some
people with mediocre talent, but with great inner
drive, go much further than people with vastly
superior talent.

Sophia Loren

God hasn't called me to be successful. He's called
me to be faithful.

Mother Teresa

Come from Your Vision

What lies behind us and what lies before us are
tiny matters compared to what lies within us.

Ralph Waldo Emerson

I shut my eyes in order to see.

Paul Gauguin

If you have built castles in the air, your work need
not be lost; that is where they should be. Now put
the foundations under them.

Henry David Thoreau

When the soul wishes to experience something she
throws an image of the experience out before her
and enters into her own image.

Meister Eckhart

Life is mostly a self-fulfilling prophecy.

Bill Hyche

If there was already a path it would have to be
someone else's. The whole point is to find your
own way.

Joseph Campbell

We lose ourselves in our love of the task before us,
and in that moment we learn an identity that lives
both within us and beyond us.

Theodeu Roszak

The future enters into us in order to transform
itself in us, long before it happens.

Rainer Maria Rilke

To see things in the seed, that is genius.

Lao-Tzu

To burn with this hard, gemlike flame, to maintain
this ecstasy, is success in life.

Walter Pater

You see things and ask "why?" But I dream things
that never were and I say "why not?"

George Bernard Shaw

How far would Moses have gone if he had taken a
poll in Egypt?

Harry Truman

He who has a why to live can bear almost any how.

Friedrich Nietzsche

What matters is not the idea a man holds, but the
depth at which he holds it.

Ezra Pound

In order to serve its purpose, a vision has to be a
shared vision.

Warren Bennis

Come from Your Heart

People are like stained glass windows: they sparkle
and shine when the sun is out, but when the
darkness sets in, their true beauty is revealed only
if there is a light within.

Elizabeth Kubler-Ross

To know what you prefer instead of humbly saying
Amen to what the world tells you you ought to
believe is to have kept your soul alive.

Robert Louis Stevenson

What I am actually saying is that we need to be
willing to let our intuition guide us, and then
be willing to follow that guidance directly
and fearlessly.

Shakti Gawain

There are two ways of spreading light: to be the
candle or the mirror that reflects it.

Edith Wharton

Follow your bliss.

Joseph Campbell

If you live for love, you spread kindness and
compassion everywhere you go. When you stop
believing in your heart, you are but a sterile vessel
wandering in the wilderness.

Francis Hegmeyer

Be really whole and all things will come to you

Lao-Tzu

Man cannot do great things. He can only do small things with great love.

Mother Theresa

Those who serve a cause are not those who love that cause. They are those who love the life which has to be had in order to serve it...except in the case of the very purest, and they are rare.

Simone Weil

What comes from the heart, goes to the heart.

Samuel Taylor Coleridge

The heart that breaks open can contain the whole universe.

Joanna Macy

Great hearts steadily send forth the secret forces that incessantly draw great events.

Ralph Waldo Emerson

Follow your heart, but be quiet for a while first. Ask questions, then feel the answer. Learn to trust your heart.

Anonymous

It is not the size of a man but the size of his heart that matters.

Evander Holyfield

Come from Abundance

You can always order another one.

Bill Hyche

I am come that they might have life, and that they
might have it more abundantly.

John 10:10

I know of no safe depository of the ultimate
powers of society but the people themselves.

Thomas Jefferson

I was given life that I may enjoy all things.

Anonymous

Anyone can count the seeds in an apple. No one
can count the apples in a seed.

Anonymous

The greatest good you can do for another is not just
to share your riches but to reveal to him his own.

Benjamin Disraeli

To live content with small means; to seek elegance
rather than luxury, and refinement rather than
fashion; to be worthy, not respectable, and wealthy,
not rich; to study hard, think quietly, talk gently,
act frankly; to listen to stars and birds, to babes
and sages, with open heart; to bear all cheerfully,
do all bravely, await occasions, hurry never. In
a word, to let the spiritual, unbidden and
unconscious, grow up through the common.
This is to be my symphony.

William Henry Channing

Everything you need you already have. You are
complete right now, you are a whole, total person,
not an apprentice person on the way to someplace
else. Your completeness must be understood by
you and experienced in your thoughts as your own
personal reality.

Wayne Dyer

When riches begin to come they come so quickly,
in such great abundance, that one wonders where
they have been hiding during all those lean years.

Napoleon Hill

You are wholly complete and your success in life
will be in direct proportion to your ability to
accept this truth about you.

Dr. Robert Anthony

My definition of success is total self-acceptance.
We can obtain all of the material possessions we
desire quite easily, however, attempting to change
our deepest thoughts and learning to love
ourselves is a monumental challenge. We may
achieve success in our business lives but it never
quite means as much if we do not feel good inside.
Once we feel good about ourselves inside we can
genuinely lend ourselves to others.

Franki

A man's life consisteth not in the abundance of the
things which he possesseth.

Luke 12:15

Make Money

The more we learn to operate in the world based
on trust in our intuition, the stronger our channel
will be and the more money we will have.

Shakti Gawain

Money, young man, is good for the nerves.

J. P. Morgan

Money and goods are certainly the best of
references.

Charles Dickens

There are few sorrows, however poignant, in which
a good income is of no avail.

Logan Pearsall Smith

Money will come when you are doing the
right thing.

Mike Phillips

When you are ready to go out to pasture—make
sure you own the pasture.

Anonymous

Money is applause.

Jacqueline Susann

Those who condemn wealth are those who have
none and see no chance of getting it.

William Penn Patrick

Work is the price you pay for money.

Anonymous

Remember that time is money.

Benjamin Franklin

Remember that credit is money.

Benjamin Franklin

A lean purse is easier to cure than endure.

George S. Clason

Watch the costs and the profits will take care
of themselves.

Aristotle

The engine which drives Enterprise is not Thrift,
but Profit.

John Maynard Keynes

Money will buy a pretty good dog but it won't buy
the wag of his tail.

Henry Wheeler Shaw

Having more money does not insure happiness.
People with ten million dollars are no happier than
people with nine million dollars.

Hobart Brown

Save Money

There is a certain Buddhistic calm from having
money in the bank.

Ayn Rand

The lack of money is the root of all evil.

George Bernard Shaw

From birth to age 18 a girl needs good parents.
From 18 to 35 she needs good looks. From 35 to 55
she needs a good personality, and from 55 on she
needs cash.

Sophie Tucker

One cannot both feast and become rich.

Ashanti Proverb

Green is the most powerful color in this country.

Andrew Young

I was brought up to believe the important thing
was not how much money you want, but how
much money you save.

Grant Hill

To be poor and independent is very nearly an
impossibility.

William Cobbett

The trouble with being poor is that it takes up all
of your time.

Willem de Kooning

The only thing money gives you is the freedom of
not worrying about money.

Johnny Carson

If your outgo exceeds your income, then your
upkeep will be your downfall.

Bill Earle

It requires a great deal of boldness and a great deal
of caution to make a great fortune, and when you
have it, it requires ten times as much skill to
keep it.

Ralph Waldo Emerson

You can't fatten the pig on market day.

John Howard

No man's credit is ever as good as his money.

Edgar Watson Howe

Whatever you have spend less.

Samuel Johnson

I've been rich and I've been poor. Rich is better.

Sophie Tucker

The shortest recorded period of time lies between
the minute you put some money away for a rainy
day and the unexpected arrival of rain.

Jane Bryant Quinn

Give Money Away

Save and invest as though you would live forever. Share and spend as though you would die tomorrow.

Jack and Lois Johnson

The man who dies rich dies disgraced.

Andrew Carnegie

Money is God in action.

Raymond Charles Baker

Let us not be satisfied with just giving money. Money is not enough, money can be got, but they need your hearts to love them. So, spread your love everywhere you go.

Mother Teresa

There is nothing wrong with men possessing riches but the wrong comes when riches possess men.

Billy Graham

Money is like manure. You have to spread it around or it smells.

J. Paul Getty

Money, it has been said, has two properties. It is flat so that it can be piled up. But it is also round so that it can circulate.

Geoffrey Crowther

For the love of money is a root of all kinds of evil.

1 Timothy 6:10

Money is like love; it kills slowly and painfully the one who withholds it, and enlivens the other who turns it on his fellow man.

Kahlil Gibran

If a person gets his attitude toward money straight, it will help straighten out almost every other area in his life.

Billy Graham

It is rare indeed that people give. Most people guard and keep; they suppose that it is they themselves and what they identify with themselves that they are guarding and keeping, whereas what they are actually guarding and keeping is their system of reality and what they assume themselves to be.

James Baldwin

It is better to give than to lend, and it costs about the same.

Philip Gibbs

Plant a kernel of wheat and you reap a pint; plant a pint and you reap a bushel. Always the law works to give you back more than you give.

Anthony Norvell

Sharing what you have is more important than what you have.

Albert M. Wells, Jr.

Keep an Open Mind

Nothing is more dangerous than an idea when it is
the only one you have.

Emile Charier

Nothing contributes more to peace of soul than
having no opinion at all.

Georg Christoph Lichtenberg

Loyalty to a petrified opinion never yet broke a
chain or freed a human soul.

Mark Twain

To fall into a habit is to begin to cease to be.

Miguel de Unamuno

It is the commonest of mistakes to consider that
the limit of our power of perception is also the
limit of all there is to perceive.

C. W. Leadbeater

A closed mind is a dying mind.

Edna Ferber

He who knows only his own side of the case,
knows little of that.

John Stuart Mill

Beware of the man of one book.

St. Thomas Aquinas

The only means of strengthening one's intellect is to make up one's mind about nothing—to let the mind be a thoroughfare for all thoughts.

John Keats

Where there is an open mind, there will always be a frontier.

Charles F. Kettering

The beautiful souls are they that are universal, open, and ready for all things.

Michel Eyquem de Montaigne

I've noticed two things about men who get big salaries. They are almost invariably men who, in conversation or in conference, are adaptable. They quickly get the other fellow's view. They are more eager to do this than to express their own ideas. Also, they state their own point of view convincingly.

John Hallock

If you never change your mind, why have one?

Edward De Bono

Just as our eyes need light in order to see, our minds need ideas in order to conceive.

Napoleon Hill

Acknowledge Differences

If you were just like me, how would I know who
you would be?

> *Camren Edison King*
> *(My four-year-old grandson)*

The meeting of two personalities is like the contact
of two chemical substances: if there is any reaction,
both are changed.

> *Carl Jung*

We may have all come on different ships, but we're
in the same boat now.

> *Martin Luther King, Jr.*

The responsibility of tolerance lies with those who
have the wider vision.

> *George Elliot*

In a real sense, all life is interrelated. All men are
caught in an inescapable network of mutuality,
tied in a single garment of destiny. Whatever
affects one directly affects all indirectly... I can
never be what I ought to be until you are what you
ought to be, and you can never be what you ought
to be until I am what I ought to be. This is the
interrelated structure of reality.

> *Martin Luther King, Jr.*

We become not a melting pot but a beautiful
mosaic. Different people, different beliefs, different
yearnings, different hopes, different dreams.

> *Jimmy Carter*

If you have learned how to disagree without being disagreeable, then you have discovered the secret of getting along—whether it be business, family relations, or life itself.

Bernard Meltzer

Most of the arguments to which I am party fall somewhat short of being impressive, knowing to the fact that neither I nor my opponent knows what we are talking about.

Robert Benchley

He who establishes his argument by noise and command shows that his reason is weak.

Michel Eyquem de Montaigne

Since the 1960s, we have seen the failure of the melting pot ideology. This ideology suggested that different historical, cultural and socioeconomic backgrounds could be subordinated to a larger ideology or social amalgam which is "America." This concept obviously did not work, because paradoxically America encourages a politics of contestation.

Charles Horton Cooley

It's the things in common that make relationships enjoyable, but it's the little differences that make them interesting.

Todd Ruthman

Acknowledge Unity

We shall be one person.

Pueblo Indian

We cannot live only for ourselves. A thousand fibers connect us with our fellow men; and among those fibers, as sympathetic threads, our actions run as causes, and they come back to us as effects.

Herman Melville

A hundred times every day I remind myself that my inner and outer life depends on the labors of other men, living and dead, and that I must exert myself in order to give in the measure as I have received and am still receiving.

Albert Einstein

Everything is connected to everything else. Everything must go somewhere. Nature knows best. There is no such thing as a free lunch.

Barry Commoner

Humankind has not woven the web of life. We are but one thread within it. Whatever we do to the web, we do to ourselves. All things are bound together. All things connect.

Chief Seattle

Here is a basic rule for winning success. Let's mark it in the mind and remember it. The rule is: success depends on the support of other people. The only hurdle between you and what you want is the support of others.

Anonymous

With all beings and all things we shall be as relatives.

Sioux Indian

Every man beareth the whole stamp of the
human condition.

Michel Eyquem de Montaigne

We must all hang together or assuredly we shall all
hang separately.

Benjamin Franklin

We must learn to live together as brothers or
perish together as fools.

Martin Luther King, Jr.

Nothing less than becoming one with the universe
will suffice.

Morihei Ueshiba

It was a beautiful, harmonious, peaceful-looking
planet, blue with white clouds, and one that gave
you a deep sense... of home, of being, of identity. It
is what I prefer to call instant global connectedness.

Edgar Mitchell, Astronaut
(Viewing earth from the moon)

We are each other's business: we are each other's
magnitude and bond.

Gwendolyn Brooks

No matter what part of the world we come from,
we are all basically the same human beings. We all
seek happiness and try to avoid suffering.

The Dalai Lama

Do Not Judge

If you judge people, you have no time to
love them.

Mother Teresa

Puritanism—the haunting fear that someone,
somewhere, may be happy.

Henry Louis Mencken

When the judgment is weak, the prejudice
is strong.

O'Hara

Prejudice is the reason of fools.

Voltaire

No person should be held to answer for every little
thing in their past. What's important is who they
are now and what they do.

Charles Garry

Do not judge lest you be judged. For in the way
you judge, you will be judged; and by your
standard of measure, it will be measured to you.

Matthew 7:1–2

Whenever you feel like criticizing anyone.... Just
remember that all the people in this world haven't
had the advantages that you've had.

F. Scott Fitzgerald

The choice to judge rather than to know is the
cause of the loss of peace.

A Course In Miracles

If you are pained by external things, it is not
they that disturb you, but your own judgment
of them. And it is in your power to wipe out
that judgment now.

Marcus Aurelius

It took me a long time not to judge myself through
someone else's eyes.

Sally Field

We judge ourselves by what we feel capable of
doing, while others judge us by what we have
already done.

Henry Wadsworth Longfellow

We need very strong ears to hear ourselves judged
frankly, and because there are few who can endure
frank criticism without being stung by it, those
who venture to criticize us perform a remarkable
act of friendship, for to undertake to wound or
offend a man for his own good is to have a healthy
love for him.

Michel Eyquem de Montaigne

Make no judgments where you have no compassion.

Anne McCarrfey

It has been my experience that folks that have no
vices have very few virtues.

Abraham Lincoln

Take Risks

There is the risk you cannot afford to take, and
there is the risk you cannot afford not to take.

Peter Drucker

The universe will reward you for taking risks on
its behalf.

Shakti Gawain

Chance is always powerful. Let your hook always
be cast; in the pool where you least expect it, there
will be a fish.

Ovid

It is not because things are difficult that we do
not dare; it is because we do not dare that they
are difficult.

Seneca, the Elder

We cannot escape fear. We can only transform it
into a companion that accompanies us on all our
exciting adventures.... Take a risk a day—one
small or one bold stroke that will make you feel
great once you have done it.

Susan Jeffers

All the best things in life come packaged in a
ribbon of risk. You untie the gift, and you assume
the risk, and equally, the joy. Parenthood is like
that. Marriage is like that. Friendship is like that. In
order to experience life in the full sense, you
expose yourself to a bottomless pit of vulnerability.
That is the essence of true love.

Kristin Armstrong

Trust that still, small voice that says, "This might work and I'll try it."

Diane Mariechild

Life is either a daring adventure or nothing.

Helen Keller

An idea that isn't risky is hardly worth calling an idea.

Oscar Wilde

Security is mostly a superstition. It does not occur in nature.

Helen Keller

Without risk, faith is impossible.

Soren Kierkegaard

The impossible is often the untried.

Jim Goodwin

Why not go out on a limb? That's where the fruit is.

Will Rogers

Take a chance! All life is a chance. The man who goes the furthest is generally the one who is willing to do and dare. The "sure thing" boat never gets far from shore.

Dale Carnegie

Follow a trail of bold mistakes and at the end of them you will find a genius.

Roy H. Williams

Take Action

In any moment of decision, the best thing you can
do is the right thing. The worst thing you can do
is nothing.

Theodore Roosevelt

Like an ability or muscle, hearing your inner
wisdom is strengthened by doing it.

Robbie Gass

Whatever God's dream about man may be,
it seems certain it cannot come true unless
man cooperates.

Stella Terrill Mann

And while I sit and beat the bush, there shall step
in other men and catch the birds.

John Heywood

Iron rusts from disuse...even so does inaction sap
the vigor of the mind.

Leonardo da Vinci

I have always thought the actions of men the best
interpreters of their thoughts.

John Locke

All the beautiful sentiments in the world weigh less
than a single lovely action.

James Russell Lowell

As I grow older, I pay less attention to what men
say. I just watch what they do.

Mae West

Before you hit the jackpot, you have to put a coin in the machine.

Flip Wilson

Man is born to live and not to prepare to live.

Boris Pasternak

Even if you're on the right track, you'll get run over if you just sit there.

Will Rogers

As the body without spirit is dead, so faith without works is dead also.

James 2:26

I am only one; but still I am one. I cannot do everything, but still I can do something; I will not refuse to do the something I can do.

Helen Keller

Our actions are all that separate our daydreams from our goals.

Roy H. Williams

Swing at the strikes.

Yogi Berra

He that lives upon hope will die fasting.

Benjamin Franklin

A knowledge of the path cannot be substituted for putting one foot in front of the other.

M. C. Richards

Aim High

If you deliberately set out to be less than you are capable of, you'll be unhappy for the rest of your life.

Abraham Maslo

Shoot for the moon. Even if you miss it, you will land among the stars.

Les Brown

There is only one success—to be able to spend your life in your own way.

Christopher Morley

Finally, brethren, whatever is true, whatever is honorable, whatever is right, whatever is pure, whatever is lovely, whatever is of good repute, if there is any excellence and if anything worthy of praise, let your mind dwell on these things.

Philippians 4:8

Some goals are so worthy, it's glorious even to fail.

Anonymous

The quality of a person's life is in direct proportion to their commitment to excellence, regardless of their chosen field of endeavor.

Vince Lombardi

There is always room at the top.

Daniel Webster

Nobody remembers who came in second.

Charles Schultz

Success is simply a matter of luck—ask any failure.

Earl Wilson

Most people live, whether physically, intellectually or morally, in a very restricted circle of their potential being. They make use of a very small portion of their possible consciousness, and of their soul's resources in general, much like a man who, out of his whole bodily organism, should get into the habit of using and moving only his little finger. Great emergencies and crises show us how much greater our vital resources are than we had supposed.

William James

Far away there in the sunshine are my highest aspirations. I may not reach them but I can look up and see their beauty, believe in them and try to follow them.

Louisa May Alcott

Reach high, for stars lie hidden in your soul.
Dream deep for every dream precedes the goal.

Pamela Vaull Starr

When you reach the top, that's when the climb begins.

Michael Caine

No more effort is required to aim high in life, to demand abundance and prosperity, than is required to accept misery and poverty.

Napoleon Hill

Be Different

Anybody who is any good is different from
anybody else.

Felix Frankfurter

Eliminate something superfluous from your life.
Break a habit. Do something that makes you feel
insecure. Carry out an action with complete
attention and intensity, as if it were your last.

Piero Ferrucci

A foolish consistency is the hobgoblin of little
minds, adored by little statesmen and philosophers
and divines. With consistency a great soul has
simply nothing to do.

Ralph Waldo Emerson

If a man does not keep pace with his companions,
perhaps it is because he hears a different drummer.
Let him keep step to the music which he hears,
however measured or far away.

Henry David Thoreau

Change does not necessarily assume progress, but
progress implacably requires change.

Henry Steele Commager

What is right for one soul may not be right for
another. It may mean having to stand on your own
and do something strange in the eyes of others.

Eileen Caddy

To be a success in business, be daring, be first,
be different.

Marchant

If you see in any given situation only what
everybody else can see, you can be said to be so
much a representative of your culture that you are
a victim of it.

S. I. Hayakawa

Conformity is the jailer of freedom and the enemy
of growth.

John F. Kennedy

Mass democracy, mass morality and the media
thrive independently of the individual who joins
them only at the cost of at least a partial perversion
of his instinct and insights. He pays for his social
ease with what used to be called his soul, his
discriminations, his uniqueness, his psychic
energy, his self.

Al Alvarez

There is only one success—to spend your life in
your own way.

Christopher Morley

In order to be irreplaceable, one must always
be different.

Coco Chanel

Work Smart

Happiness lies in the absorption of some vocation
which satisfies the soul.

Henry Ward Beecher

Nobody ever drowned in sweat.

Anonymous

Most men would feel insulted if it were proposed
to employ them in throwing stones over a wall,
and then in throwing them back merely that they
might earn their wages. But many are no more
worthily employed now.

Henry David Thoreau

Work is love made visible.

Khalil Gibran

There is dignity in work only when it is work
freely accepted.

Albert Camus

Genius is one percent inspiration and ninety-nine
percent perspiration.

Thomas Edison

Pleasure in the job puts perfection in the work.

Aristotle

I'm a great believer in luck, and I find the harder I
work the more of it I have.

Thomas Jefferson

Thunder is good. Thunder is impressive. But it is
the lightening that does the work.

Mark Twain

Your diamonds are not in far distant mountains or
in yonder seas; they are in your own backyard, if
you but dig for them.

Russell H. Conwell

Bless thee in all the work of thy hand which
thou doest.

Deuteronomy 14:29

The only place where success comes before work is
in the dictionary.

Vidal Sasson

The harder you work, the luckier you get.

Gary Player

The more I want to get something done, the less I
call it work.

Richard Bach

Opportunities are usually disguised by hard work,
so most people don't recognize them.

Ann Landers

Luck is what happens when preparation
meets opportunity.

Darrel Royal

Have Fun

You will hereafter be called to account for
depriving yourself of the good things which the
world lawfully allows.

The Talmud

You can discover more about a person in an hour
of play than in a year of conversation.

Plato

Thought is the labor of the intellect; reverie is
its pleasure.

Victor Hugo

Man is most nearly himself when he achieves the
seriousness of a child at play.

Heraclitus

And the people sat down to eat and to drink, and
rose up to play.

Exodus 32:6

The true object of life is play.

G. K. Chesterton

Without this playing with fantasy, no creative work
has ever yet come to birth. The debt we owe to the
play of imagination is incalculable.

Carl Jung

In every real man a child is hidden that wants
to play.

Friedrich Nietzsche

My only regret in life is that I did not drink
more champagne.

John Maynard Keynes

Play is the exultation of the possible.

Martin Buber

Joy is not in things, it is in us.

Wagner

No man is a failure who is enjoying life.

William Feather

A little nonsense now and then is treasured by the
best of men.

Phil Donahue

A person has two legs and one sense of humor, and
if faced with the choice, it's better to lose a leg.

Charles Lindner

All animals except man know that the ultimate of
life is to enjoy it.

Samuel Butler

People rarely succeed unless they have fun in what
they are doing.

Dale Carnegie

Be Happy

Happiness makes up in height for what it lacks
in length.

Robert Frost

At the height of laughter, the universe is flung into
a kaleidoscope of new possibilities.

Jean Houston

Always leave enough time in your life to do
something that makes you happy, satisfied, or even
joyous. That has more of an effect on economic
well-being than any other single factor.

Paul Hawken

I have no money, no resources, no hopes. I am the
happiest man alive.

Henry Miller

The vigorous, the healthy and the happy survive
and multiply.

Charles Darwin

That is happiness; to be dissolved into something
complete and great.

Willa Sibert Cather

Happiness is not having what you want but
wanting what you have.

Dr. Hyman Judah Schactel

Happiness is a warm puppy.

Charles Schultz

Most people are about as happy as they make up their minds to be.

Abraham Lincoln

A happy person is not a person in a certain set of circumstances, but rather a person with a certain set of attitudes.

Hugh Downs

Always laugh when you can. It's cheap medicine.

Lord Byron

Satisfaction of one's curiosity is one of the greatest sources of happiness in life.

Linus Pauling

There are some days I think I am going to die from an overdose of satisfaction.

Salvador Dali

Humor is a prelude to faith and laughter and is the beginning of prayer.

Reinhold Niebuhr

People don't notice whether it's winter or summer when they're happy.

Anton Chekhov

All the things I like to do are either immoral, illegal or fattening.

Alexander Woolcott

Embrace Mystery

I do not know whether I was then a man dreaming
I was a butterfly, or whether I am now a butterfly
dreaming I am a man.

Chuang-Tzu

Physical concepts are the creations of the human
mind, and are not, however it may seem,
determined by the external world. In our endeavor
to understand reality we are somewhat like a man
trying to understand the mechanism of a closed
watch. He can see the hands move and hear its
ticking but he has no way of opening the case. If he
is ingenious, he may form some picture of a
mechanism, which could be responsible for all the
things he observes but he will never be quite sure
his picture is the only one which could explain his
observation. He will never be able to compare his
pictures with the real mechanism and he cannot
even imagine the meaning of such a comparison.

Albert Einstein

It is only when we realize that life is taking us
nowhere that it begins to have meaning.

P. D. Ouspensky

What a strange machine man is! You fill him with
bread, wine, fish and radishes and out comes sighs,
laughter and dreams.

Nikos Kazantzakis
Zorba the Greek

I moved further and further away from the
conventional certainties by which social life is
illuminated.... At each step of the descent a new

person was disclosed within me.... And when I
had stopped my exploration because the path faded
beneath my steps, I found a bottomless abyss at my
feet, and out of it came—arising I know not from
where—the current which I dare to call my life.

Teilliard de Chardin

The power lies in the wisdom and understanding
in one's role in the Great Mystery, and in honoring
every living thing as a teacher.

Jamie Sands and David Carson

To know that what is impenetrable to us really
exist, manifesting itself as the highest wisdom and
the most radiant beauty...this knowledge, this
feeling is at the center of true religiousness.

Albert Einstein

Alice laughed. "There's no use trying," she said.
"One can't believe impossible things."
"I daresay you haven't had much practice," said the
Queen. "When I was your age, I always did it for
half an hour a day. Why, sometimes, I've believed
as many as six impossible things before breakfast."

Lewis Carroll
Through the Looking Glass

There is something precious in our being mysteries
to ourselves, in our being unable ever to see
through even the person who is closest to our
heart and to reckon with him as though he were a
logical proposition or a problem in accounting.

Rudolf Bultmann

Welcome All Experiences

Everything that happens to you is your teacher.
The secret is to learn to sit at the feet of your own
life and be taught by it.

Polly B. Berends

Do not weep; do not wax indignant. Understand.

Baruch Spinoza

There would be no such a thing as counterfeit gold
if there was no real gold somewhere.

Old Sufi Proverb

Genuine beginnings begin within us, even when
they are brought to our attention by external
opportunities.

William Bridges

There is a time for everything, and a season for
every activity under heaven.

Ecclesiastes 3:1

In a dark time, the eye begins to see.

Theodore Roethke

In the middle of the journey of our life, I came to
myself within a dark wood where the straight way
was lost.

Dante Alighieri

Rough waters mean good fishing.

Cuban Proverb

Toto, I don't think we're in Kansas anymore.

Dorothy
The Wizard of Oz

This is courage...to bear unflinchingly what
heaven sends.

Euripides

When you lose, don't lose the lesson.

The Dalai Lama

The marvelous richness of human experience
would lose something of rewarding joy if there
were no limitations to overcome. The hilltop hour
would not be half so wonderful if there were no
dark valleys to traverse.

Helen Keller

Adversity introduces a man to himself.

Anonymous

All sunshine makes the desert.

Arabian Proverb

A failure is a man who has blundered, but is not
able to cash in on the experience.

Elbert Hubbard

Leaders learn by leading, and they learn best by
leading in the face of obstacles. As weather shapes
mountains, problems shape leaders.

Warren Bennis

Ask Questions

You can tell whether a man is clever by his answers.
You can tell whether a man is wise by his
questions.

Naguib Mahfouz

Monks and scholars should not accept my works
out of respect, but upon analyzing it as a
goldsmith analyzes gold, through cutting, melting,
scraping and rubbing it.

Buddha

Look and you will find it—what is unsought will
go undetected.

Sophocles

It is better to sleep on things beforehand than lie
awake about them afterward.

Baltasar Gracian

Who is the slayer, who the victim? Speak.

Sophocles

Life was meant to be lived, and curiosity must be
kept alive. One must never, for any reason, turn
one's back on life.

Eleanor Roosevelt

Ask, and it shall be given you; seek, and you shall
find; knock, and it shall be opened unto you. For
everyone who asks receives, and he who seeks
finds, and to him who knocks it shall be opened

Matthew 7:11

I'm not smart. I try to observe. Millions saw the
apple fall but Newton was the one who asked why.

Bernard Mannes Baruch

The trouble with life isn't that there is no answer,
it's that there are so many answers.

Ruth Benedict

The important thing is not to stop questioning.
Curiosity has its own reason for existing.
One cannot help but be in awe when he
contemplates the mysteries of eternity, of life, of
the marvelous structure of reality. It is enough if
one tries merely to comprehend a little of this
mystery every day. Never lose a holy curiosity.

Albert Einstein

A prudent question is one-half of wisdom.

Francis Bacon

Quality questions create a quality life. Successful
people ask better questions, and as a result, they
get better answers.

Anthony Robbins

Question with boldness even the existence of a
God; because, if there be one, he must more
approve of the homage of reason, than that of
blindfolded fear.

Thomas Jefferson

Don't Complain

My dear, I don't care what they do, so long as they don't do it in the street and frighten the horses.

Mrs. Patrick Campbell

Things without remedy should be without regard: what's done is done.

William Shakespeare

The anvil outlasts the hammer.

Anonymous

I find doing the will of God leaves me no time for disputing about His plans.

MacDonald

I joked about every prominent man in my lifetime, but I never met one I didn't like.

Will Rogers

If you want total security, go to prison. There you are fed, clothed, given medical care and so on. The only thing lacking is freedom.

Dwight Eisenhower

Some people are always grumbling that roses have thorns, I am thankful that thorns have roses.

Alphonse Karr

It is the growling man who lives a dog's life.

Coleman Cox

There is no good in arguing with the inevitable.
The only argument available with an east wind is
to put on your overcoat.

James Russell Lowell

This is the true joy in life, the being used for a
purpose recognized by yourself as a mighty one;
the being thoroughly worn out before you are
thrown on the scrap heap; the being a force of
nature instead of a feverish selfish little clod of
ailments and grievances complaining that the
world will not devote itself to making you happy.

George Bernard Shaw

Over the piano was printed a notice: Please do not
shoot the pianist. He is doing his best.

Oscar Wilde

Never regret. If it's good, it's wonderful. If it's bad,
it's experience.

Anonymous

The sun was shining in my eyes, and I could barely
see to do the necessary task that was allotted me.
Resentment of the vivid glow I started to
complain. When all at once upon the air I heard
the blind man's cane.

Earl Musselman

Be Humble

It's amazing what can be accomplished when you don't care who gets the credit.

John Wooden

To know that you do not know is the best. To pretend to know when you do not know is disease.

Lao-Tzu

Man is certainly crazy. He could not make a mite, and he makes gods by the dozen.

Michel Eyquem de Montaigne

Pride goeth before destruction, and a haughty spirit before a fall.

Proverbs 16:18

Life is a long lesson in humility.

Sir James Matthew Barrie

In vain I have looked for a single man capable of seeing his faults and bringing the charge home against himself.

Confucius

The little I know, I owe to my ignorance.

Sacha Guitry

The true leader is always led.

Carl Jung

A crown is merely a hat that lets the rain in.

Frederick the Great

The first problem for all of us, men and women, is not to learn, but to unlearn.

Gloria Steinem

After the game, the king and the pawn go into the same box.

Italian Proverb

He blows his horn so loudly; he hasn't any wind left for the climb.

Pat O'Haire

The paths of glory lead but to the grave, but so do all other paths.

George Will

We don't know one millionth of one percent about anything.

Thomas Edison

When you're as great as I am, its hard to be humble.

Muhammad Ali

Watch how a man takes praise and there you have the measure of him.

Thomas Burke

Alas, I know if I ever became truly humble, I would be proud of it.

Benjamin Franklin

Be Willing to Change

There is no sin punished more implacably by
nature than the sin of resistance to change.

Anne Morrow Lindberg

Affirmations are like prescriptions for certain
aspects of yourself you want to change.

Jerry Frankhauser

To learn is to change. Education is a process that
changes the learner.

George Leonar

Lord grant me the ability to change what I can
change, the ability to accept what I can't, and the
wisdom to know the difference.

AA Prayer

Instead of hating the people you think are
warmongers, hate the appetites and disorder in
your own soul, which are the causes of war.

Thomas Merton

All graduations in human development mean the
abandonment of a familiar position. All growth
must come to terms with this fact.

Erik H. Srikson

Unless we change our direction, we are likely to
end up where we are headed.

Chinese Proverb

Things don't change. You change your way of looking, that's all.

Carlos Castaneda

The only person who likes change is a wet baby.

Roy Z-M Blitzer

In spite of illness, in spite even of the archenemy sorrow, one can remain alive long past the usual date of disintegration if one is unafraid of change, insatiable in intellectual curiosity, interested in big things, and happy in small ways.

Edith Wharton

Your life is going to be as interesting as you make it. Keep active. Keep working. Keep trying. And don't be afraid of change.

Delores Hope

Keep changing. When you are through changing you are through.

Bruce Barton

They must often change, who would be constant in happiness or wisdom.

Confucius

Change cannot be avoided.... Change provides the opportunities for innovation. It gives you the chance to demonstrate your creativity.

Keshavan Nair

Be Willing to Accept

Life is not the way it's supposed to be. It's the way
it is. The way you cope with it is what makes
the difference.

Virginia Satir

Nevertheless the flowers fall with our attachment
and the weeds spring up with our aversion.

Dogen

The more things change, the more they stay the same.

Alphonse Karr

Oh, East is East, and West is West, and never the
twain shall meet.

Rudyard Kipling

So I awoke, and behold it was a dream.

John Bunyan

Expect nothing; live frugally on surprise.

Alice Walker

When an inner situation is not made conscious, it
appears outside as fate.

Carl Jung

Truth is what stands the test of experience.

Albert Einstein

Make it a rule of life never to regret and never look
back. Regret is an appalling waste of energy; you
can't build on it; it is good only for wallowing in.

Katherine Mansfield

My job is not to change anyone. My job is to
awaken myself.

Bill Hyche

It's no use in crying over spilt milk. It only makes it
salty for the cat.

Anonymous

The man who has no problems is out of the game.

Elbert Hubbard

A dog is a dog except when he is facing you. Then
he is Mr. Dog.

Haitian Farmer

Would you rather be right or happy?

Jerry Jampolosky

Girls grow up and become adults. Boys just get
taller.

Roy H. Williams

In the face of an obstacle which is impossible to
overcome, stubbornness is stupid.

Simone de Beauvoir

One half of the world cannot understand the
pleasures of the other.

Jane Austen

God grant me the serenity to accept the things I
cannot change, the courage to change the things I
can, and the wisdom to know the difference.

Reinhold Niebuhr

Make Peace

Nonviolence is the first article of my faith. It is also
the last article of my creed.

Mahatma Gandhi

Anger is the wind which blows out the lamp of
the mind.

Robert Ingersoll

Blessed are the peacemakers, for they shall be
called sons of God.

Matthew 5:9

Henceforth the adequacy of any military
establishment will be tested by its ability to
preserve the peace.

Henry Kissinger

All anger is an attempt to make someone feel guilty.

A Course in Miracles

We train in hopes of being of some use, however
small our role may be, in the task of bringing peace
to mankind around the world.

Morihei Ueshiba

With malice toward none, with charity for all…let
us finish the work we are in, to bind up the
nation's wounds.

Abraham Lincoln

When women have a voice in national and
international affairs, war will cease forever.

Augusta Stowe-Gullen

When faced with angry conflict, it is easy to get lost in the issues and lose sight of the fact that any form of peacemaking is a commitment to a self-inquiring process of communication. How I / you / we relate to the issues is the deeper issue when faced with conflict. Within this process, I am discovering that my own anger can be transmuted into passion when I reframe my relationship with the issues—from what I am fighting against to what I am prepared to stand up for. And what I am willing to stand up (and speak out) for is my faith in the innate goodness in human beings, our willingness and desire to strive toward a peaceful coexistence and our infinite capacity for growth.

Julie Knowles

I think that people want peace so much that one of these days government had better get out of their way and let them have it.

Dwight D. Eisenhower

Peace, like freedom, is no original state which existed from the start; we shall have to make it, in the truest sense of the word.

Willy Brandt

Everybody today seems to be in such a terrible rush, anxious for greater developments and greater riches and so on, so that children have very little time for their parents. Parents have very little time for each other, and in the home begins the disruption of peace of the world.

Mother Teresa

Keep It Simple

The art of art, the glory of expression, and the sunshine of the light of letters is simplicity.

Walt Whitman

During the space race, the U.S. spent $2 million developing a pen that would write in zero gravity. The Russians solved the same problem with a 5-cent pencil.

Anonymous

True eloquence consist in saying all that is necessary, and nothing but what is necessary.

La Rochefoucauld

The wisdom of life consists in the elimination of nonessentials.

Lin Yutang

Simplicity is the soul of efficiency.

Richard Austin Freeman

It was beautiful and simple as all truly great swindles are.

O. Henry

Perhaps too much of everything is as bad as too little.

Edna Ferber

Nothing is so simple that it cannot be misunderstood.

Jr. Teague

The ability to simplify means to eliminate the unnecessary so that the necessary may speak.

Hans Hofmann

The trouble with so many of us is that we underestimate the power of simplicity. We have a tendency it seems to over complicate our lives and forget what's important and what's not. We tend to mistake movement for achievement. We tend to focus on activities instead of results. And as the pace of life continues to race along in the outside world, we forget that we have the power to control our lives regardless of what's going on outside.

Robert Stuberg

We struggle with the complexities and avoid the simplicities.

Norman Vincent Peale

I believe that a simple and unassuming manner of life is best for everyone, best for both the body and the mind.

Albert Einstein

Eat when you're hungry. Drink when you're thirsty. Sleep when you're tired.

Buddhist Proverb

Simplicity is the ultimate sophistication.

Leonardo da Vinci

Live in the Present

The work will wait while you show the child the
rainbow; but the rainbow won't wait while you do
the work.

Patricia Clafford

I think it pisses God off if you walk by the color
purple in a field somewhere and don't notice it.

Alice Walker

What a wonderful life I have had! I only wish I had
realized it sooner.

Colette

Write in your heart that every day is the best day
of the year.

Ralph Waldo Emerson

As the generation of leaves, so is that of men.

Homer

I like living. I have sometimes been wildly,
despairingly, acutely miserable, racked with
sorrow, but through it all I still know quite
certainly that just to be alive is a grand thing.

Agatha Christie

Sometimes I would almost rather have people take
away years of my life than take away a moment.

Pearle Bailey

It is better to live rich than to die rich.

Samuel Johnson

When one door closes, another door opens; but we often look so long and regretfully upon the closed door that we do not see the ones which open.

Alexander Graham Bell

Let others praise ancient times; I am glad I was born in these.

Ovid

Light tomorrow with today.

Elizabeth Barrett Browning

Life is a succession of moments. To live each one is to succeed.

Corita Kent

The "what should be" never did exist, but people keep trying to live up to it. There is no "what should be," there's only what is.

Lenny Bruce

Dwell not on the past. Use it to illustrate a point, then leave it behind. Nothing really matters except what you do now in this instant of time. From this moment onwards you can be an entirely different person, filled with love and understanding, ready with an outstretched hand, uplifted and positive in every thought and deed.

Eileen Caddy

Dance

I don't want people who want to dance; I want people who have to dance.

George Balanchine

Music attracts the angels in the universe.

Bob Dylan

You will do foolish things, but do them with enthusiasm.

Colette

Those who wish to sing always find a song.

Swedish Proverb

We look at the dance to impart the sensation of living in an affirmation of life, to energize the spectator into keener awareness of the vigor, the mystery, the humor, the variety, and the wonder of life. This is the function of the American dance.

Martha Graham

Music and rhythm find their way into the secret places of the soul.

Plato

The hills and the sea and the earth dance. The world of man dances in laughter and tears.

Kabir

Dance is the only art of which we ourselves are the stuff of which it is made.

Ted Shawn

Dancing is a perpendicular expression of a
horizontal desire.

George Bernard Shaw

Would you sell the colors of your sunset and the
fragrance of your flowers, and the passionate
wonder of your forest for a creed that will not let
you dance?

Helene Johnson

Remember, Ginger Rogers did everything Fred
Astaire did, but she did it backwards and in
high heels.

Faith Whittlesey

And when you get the chance to sit it out or dance,
I hope you dance.

LeeAnn Womack
(CD—I Hope You Dance)

I could dance with you until the cows come home.
Better still, I'll dance with the cows till *you*
come home.

Groucho Marx

I dance not to entertain but to help people better
understand each other.... Because through dance I
have experienced the wordless joy of freedom, I
seek it more fully now for my people and for all
people everywhere.

Pearl Primus

Dream

The future belongs to those who believe in
their dreams.

Eleanor Roosevelt

Go confidently in the direction of your dreams!
Live the life you have imagined. As you simplify
your life, the laws of the universe will be simpler.

Henry David Thoreau

Ah, but a man's reach should exceed his grasp, or
what's a heaven for?

Robert Browning

It is good to have an end to journey toward, but it
is the journey that matters in the end.

Ursula K. LeGuin

Imagination is more important than knowledge.

Albert Einstein

The world is but a canvas to our imagination.

Henry David Thoreau

Behold, this dreamer cometh.

Genesis 37:19

Man is not the sum of what he has but the totality
of what he does not yet have, of what he
might have.

Jean-Paul Sartre

Dream, diversify and never miss an angle.

Walt Disney

But a man who doesn't dream is like a man who doesn't sweat. He stores up a lot of poison.

Truman Capote

When you cease to dream you cease to live.

Malcolm Forbes

It may be those who do most, dream most.

Stephen Leacock

I like the dreams of the future better than the history of the past.

Thomas Jefferson

Let a man listen to his dream so he may hear the story of all men and let him say as he did when he was a child: this is true; it does not matter what they tell me.

William Wantling

You gotta have a dream. If you don't have a dream, how ya gonna make a dream come true?

Bloody Mary
South Pacific

I have a dream that my four little children will one day live in a nation where they will not be judged by the color of their skin but by the content of their character.

Martin Luther King, Jr.

Be Creative

The great creative individual...is capable of more
wisdom and virtue than collective man ever
can be.

John Stuart Mill

Every child is an artist. The problem is how to
remain an artist once he grows up.

Pablo Picasso

As an artist it is central to be unsatisfied! This isn't
greed, though it might be appetite.

Lawrence Calcagno

The world of reality has its limits; the world of
imagination is boundless.

Jean-Jacques Rousseau

There is a logic of colors, and it is with this alone,
and not the logic of the brain, that the painter
should conform.

Paul Cézanne

Only when he no longer knows what he is doing
does the painter do good things.

Edgar Degas

Art? You just do it.

Martin Ritt

The function of the creative artist consists of
making laws, not in following laws already made.

Ferruccio Busoni

The job of the artist is always to deepen the mystery.

Francis Bacon

The creation of something new is not
accomplished by the intellect but by the play
instinct acting from inner necessity. The creative
mind plays with the objects it loves.

Carl Jung

No amount of skillful invention can replace the
essential element of imagination.

Edward Hopper

But if you have nothing at all to create, then
perhaps you create yourself.

Carl Jung

The work of art which I do not make, none other
will ever make.

Simone Weil

To live a creative life we must lose our fear of
being wrong.

Joseph Chilton Pearce

Living in process is being open to insight and
encounter. Creativity is becoming intensively
absorbed in the process and giving it form.

Susan Smith

Creative intelligence in its various forms and
activities is what makes man.

James Harvey Robinson

Be Authentic

I am not bound to win; I am bound to be true. I am not bound to succeed, but I am bound to live up to the light I have.

Abraham Lincoln

Children are unpredictable. You never know what inconsistency they're going to catch you in next.

Franklin P. Jones

When we are plateaued, we are not so much actively unhappy as we are just not happy. We could continue to live as we are, because usually it is not awful. But it is also not joyous. Most of us do not make changes in our lives until the pain in the present eclipses our fear of the future.

Judith M. Bardwick

To be nobody-but-yourself—in a world which is doing its best, night and day, to make you everybody else—means to fight the hardest battle which any human being can fight; and never stop fighting.

e. e. cummings

Life means for us constantly to transform into light and flame all that we are or meet with.

Friedrich Nietzsche

Twenty years from now you will be more disappointed by the things that you didn't do than by the ones you did do. So throw off the bowlines. Sail away from the safe harbor. Catch the trade winds in your sails. Explore. Dream. Discover.

Mark Twain

Many a businessman feels himself the prisoner of the commodities he sells; he has a feeling of fraudulency about this project and a secret contempt for it. Most important of all, he hates himself, because he sees his life passing him by without making any sense beyond the momentary intoxication of success.

Erich Fromm

The secret of man's being is not only to live but to have something to live for.

Dostoyevsky

I'm working all day and I'm working all night to be good-looking, healthy, and wise. And adored, content, brave, and well-read. And a marvelous hostess, fantastic in bed. And bilingual, athletic, artistic—Won't someone please stop me?

Judith Viorst

People travel to wonder at the height of mountains, and they pass by themselves without wondering.

St. Augustine

Follow your desire as long as you live; do not lessen the time of following desire, for the wasting of time is an abomination to the spirit.

Ptahhotpe, 2350 B.C.

It is the chiefest point of happiness that a man is willing to be what he is.

Desiderius Erasmus

Love Unconditionally

Some day after we have mastered the winds, the
waves, the tides and gravity, we shall harness the
energies of love. Then, for the second time in the
history of the world, man will have discovered fire.

Teilhard de Chardin

Great love can both take hold and let go.

O. R. Orage

Without love the acquisition of knowledge only
increases confusion and leads to self-destruction.

Krishnamurti

Love is the pursuit of the whole.

Plato

Children can be conceptualized as mirrors. If love
is given to them, they return it. If none is given,
they have none to return. Unconditional love is
reflected unconditionally, and conditional love is
returned conditionally.

Ross Campbell, M.D.

There is a love like a small lamp, which goes out
when the oil is consumed; or like a stream which
dries up when it doesn't rain. But there is a love
like a mighty spring gushing up out of the earth; it
keeps flowing forever, and is inexhaustible.

Isaac of Nineveh

There should be a balance between material and
spiritual progress, a balance achieved by the
principles based on love and compassion. Love and
compassion are the essence of all religion.

The Dalai Lama

Loves cures people—both the ones who give it and the ones who receive it.

Dr. Karl Menninger

Agape means nothing sentimental or basically affectionate; it means understanding, redeeming good will for all men, an overflowing love which seeks nothing in return. It is the love of God working in the lives of men. When we love on the agape level, we love men not because we like them, not because their attitudes and ways appeal to us, but because God loves them. Here we rise to the position of loving the person who does the evil deed while hating the deed he does.

Martin Luther King, Jr.

Eventually you will come to understand that love heals everything, and love is all there is.

Gary Zukav

There is a land of the living and a land of the dead and the bridge is love.

Thornton Wilder

Love doesn't make the world go around. Love is what makes the ride worthwhile.

Franklin P. Jones

Absence is to love what wind is to fire; it extinguishes the small, it inflames the great.

Bussy-Rabutin

Darkness cannot drive out darkness; only light can do that. Hate cannot drive out hate; only love can do that.

Martin Luther King, Jr.

Never Attack

When you are angry, is it not because someone has
failed to fill the function you have allotted him?
And does not this become the *reason* your attack
is justified?

A Course in Miracles

You can't hold a man down without staying down
with him.

Booker T. Washington

He who slings mud generally loses ground.

Adlai Stevenson

If you admit that to silence your opponent by force
is to win an intellectual argument, then you admit
the right to silence people by force.

Hans Eysenck

A man convinced against his will is not convinced.

Laurence J. Peter

The inclination to aggression...constitutes the
greatest impediment to civilization.

Sigmund Freud

There never was a time when, in my opinion, some
way could not be found to prevent the drawing of
the sword.

Ulysses S. Grant

Force is not a remedy.

John Bright

Today the real test of power is not capacity to make war but capacity to prevent it.

Anne O'Hare McCormick

Never think that war, no matter how necessary, nor how justified, is not a crime.

Ernest Hemingway

In some cases, non-violence requires more militancy than violence.

Cesar Chavez

You will fear what you attack.

A Course in Miracles

We know our cause is just. Because violence can only breed more violence and suffering, our struggle must remain non-violent and free of hatred. We are trying to end the suffering of our people, not to inflict suffering on others.

The Dalai Lama

Holding on to anger is like grasping a hot coal with the intent of throwing it at someone else; you are the one getting burned.

Buddha

Never Fear

What prepares you for death enhances life.

Stephen Levine

I have nothing to offer but blood, toil, tears
and sweat.

Winston Churchill

There's nothing I'm afraid of like scared people.

Robert Frost

Who is more foolish, the child afraid of the dark or
the man afraid of the light?

Maurice Freehill

To hate and to fear is to be psychologically ill. It is,
in fact, the great illness of our time.

H. A. Overstreet

You gain strength, experience and confidence by
every experience where you really stop to look
fear in the face.... You must do the thing you
cannot do.

Eleanor Roosevelt

The greatest mistake you can make is to be
continually fearing you will make one.

Elbert Hubbard

When I am afraid, I put my trust in thee.

Psalm 56:3

The only thing we have to fear is fear itself—
nameless, unreasoning, unjustified terror which
paralyzes needed efforts to convert retreat
into advance.

Franklin D. Roosevelt

We cannot escape fear. We can only transform it
into a companion that accompanies us on all our
exciting adventures. Take a risk a day—one small
or bold stroke that will make you feel great once
you have done it.

Susan Jeffers

Do not fear mistakes—there are none.

Miles Davis

Cowardly dogs bark loudest.

John Webster

There is perhaps nothing so bad and so dangerous
in life as fear.

Jawaharlal Nehru

The only real stumbling block is fear of failure. In
cooking, you've got to have a what-the-hell attitude.

Julia Child

Don't be afraid your life will end; be afraid that it
will never begin.

Grace Hansen

Trust Yourself

As soon as you trust yourself, you will know how
to live.

Goethe

We will discover the nature of our particular
genius when we stop trying to conform to our own
or to other peoples' models, learn to be ourselves,
and allow our natural channel to open.

Shakti Gawain

Trust in yourself. Your perceptions are often far
more accurate than you are willing to believe.

Claudia Black

I will be a man among men; and longer a dreamer
among shadows. Henceforth be mine a life of
action and reality! I will work in my own sphere,
nor wish it other than it is. This alone is health
and happiness.

Henry Wadsworth Longfellow

I have only two rules which I regard as principles
of conduct. The first is: have no rules. The second
is: be independent of the opinion of others.

Albert Einstein

I don't know the key to success, but the key to
failure is trying to please everybody.

Bill Cosby

If your happiness depends on what somebody else
does...you do have a problem.

Richard Bach

Life if like playing the violin in public and learning
the instrument as one goes on.

Samuel Butler

I am what I am. To look for "reasons" is beside
the point.

Joan Didion

I believe, first of all, in God, and next to all, in
Mary McLeod Bethune.

Mary McLeod Bethune

Depend on none but yourself.

Charles V

The more faithfully you listen to the voice within
you, the better you will hear what is sounding
outside. Only he who listens can speak.

Dag Hammarskjold

Every time you don't follow your inner guidance,
you feel a loss of energy, loss of power, a sense of
spiritual deadness.

Shakti Gawain

If you do not ask yourself what it is you know, you
will go on listening to others and change will not
come because you will not hear your own truth.

Saint Bartholomew

Love Yourself

Since you are like no other being ever created since
the beginning of time, you are incomparable.

Brenda Ueland

Never forget that the most powerful force on earth
is love.

Nelson A. Rockefeller

To love oneself is the beginning of a lifelong romance.

Oscar Wilde

How many cares one looses when one decides not
to be something but to be someone.

Coco Chanel

Paradise is where I am.

Voltaire

Until you make peace with who you are, you'll
never be content with what you have.

Doris Mortman

Always be a first-rate version of yourself, instead of
a second-rate version of somebody else.

Judy Garland

When we truly care for ourselves, it becomes
possible to care far more profoundly about other
people. The more alert and sensitive we are to our
own needs, the more loving and generous we can
be toward others.

Eda LeShan

Love yourself first and everything else falls into
line. You really have to love yourself to get
anything done in this world.

> *Lucille Ball*

It's easy to live for others; everybody does. I call on
you to live for yourselves.

> *Ralph Waldo Emerson*

Respect yourself if you would have others
respect you.

> *Baltasar Gracian*

Don't compromise yourself. You are all you've got.

> *Janis Joplin*

If you have anything really valuable to contribute
to the world, it will come through the expression
of your own personality, that single spark of
divinity that sets off and makes you different from
every other living creature.

> *Bruce Barton*

If God had wanted me otherwise, he would have
created me otherwise.

> *Johann von Goethe*

Your problem is you're too busy holding onto
your unworthiness.

> *Ram Dass*

Be Yourself

What I am is good enough if I would only be
it openly.

Carl Rogers

Nothing has a stronger influence psychologically
on their environment and especially on their
children than the unlived lives of the parent.

Carl Jung

If I am not for myself, who is for me? And when I
am for myself, what am I? And if not now, when?

Hillel

Often people attempt to live their lives backwards:
they try to have more things, or more money, in
order to do more of what they want so that they
will be happier. The way it actually works is the
reverse. You must first be who you really are,
then, do what you need to do, in order to have
what you want.

Margaret Young

Until you make peace with who you are, you'll
never be content with what you have.

Doris Mortman

The mother who gives up her life for her children
does them no kindness but rather burdens them
with the legacy of a life unlived.

Janet Fulldron

Nearly all men can withstand adversity, but if you want to test a man's character, give him power.

Abraham Lincoln

But if a man happens to find himself, he has a mansion which he can inhabit with dignity all the days of his life.

James Michener

It doesn't happen all at once.... You become. It takes a long time.

Margery Williams

In the world to come, I shall not be asked, "Why were you not Moses?" I should be asked, "Why were you not Zusya?"

Rabbi Zusya

When we are really honest with ourselves, we must admit our lives are all that really belong to us. So it is how we live our lives that determines the kind of men we are.

Cesar Chavez

He who knows others is wise; he who knows himself is enlightened.

Lao-Tzu

What is a man's first duty? The answer's brief: To be himself.

Henrik Icahn

About Bill Hyche

Bill Hyche is an artist, entrepreneur, professional speaker and businessman. He has co-founded and sold several high tech companies in the health care industry. He assists charitable organizations in their fundraising activities, is a professional speaker, and promotes *The Right Moment* as a gift for teachers, a corporate gift item and a fundraising resource.

Bill enjoys running, golf, his grandchildren and is currently writing a sequel to *The Right Moment* on the topic of relationships. He and his wife, Lenora, live in Austin, Texas.

Book Order Information

If you would like to purchase additional copies of *The Right Moment*, or its companion poster, please visit our web site at *www.iloveteachers.com*.

We are collecting quotations for a sequel to *The Right Moment*. If you have a favorite quotation that you would like to share with us, please e-mail it to *quotes@commongoodpress.com* or send it to our mailing address.

Most of the quotations in *The Right Moment* were collected from various sources like books, friends, newspapers, magazines, and the Internet. To the best of our knowledge, all the quotations are stated accurately and the original authors have been credited properly. For those quotations that we couldn't verify the source, we labeled them as "Anonymous." If you notice any quotations or attributions that are incorrect, please e-mail us at *quotes@commongoodpress.com* or send us your comments.

To contact the author, you may e-mail him at:
bill@commongoodpress.com

Our mailing address is:
Common Good Press
P.O. Box 341135
Austin, TX 78734

Our web site is:

www.iloveteachers.com

Finally, thank you for the contribution you are to our children and to our communities.

The End

You have delighted us long enough.

Jane Austen